Cambridge Elements

Elements in Comparative Political Behavior
edited by
Raymond Duch
University of Oxford
Anja Neundorf
University of Glasgow
Randy Stevenson
Rice University

MASS POLARIZATION ACROSS TIME AND SPACE

Isaac D. Mehlhaff
The University of Chicago

Shaftesbury Road, Cambridge CB2 8EA, United Kingdom

One Liberty Plaza, 20th Floor, New York, NY 10006, USA

477 Williamstown Road, Port Melbourne, VIC 3207, Australia

314–321, 3rd Floor, Plot 3, Splendor Forum, Jasola District Centre, New Delhi – 110025, India

103 Penang Road, #05–06/07, Visioncrest Commercial, Singapore 238467

Cambridge University Press is part of Cambridge University Press & Assessment, a department of the University of Cambridge.

We share the University's mission to contribute to society through the pursuit of education, learning and research at the highest international levels of excellence.

www.cambridge.org
Information on this title: www.cambridge.org/9781009578523

DOI: 10.1017/9781009350662

© Isaac D. Mehlhaff 2025

This publication is in copyright. Subject to statutory exception and to the provisions of relevant collective licensing agreements, no reproduction of any part may take place without the written permission of Cambridge University Press & Assessment.

When citing this work, please include a reference to the DOI 10.1017/9781009350662

First published 2025

A catalogue record for this publication is available from the British Library.

ISBN 978-1-009-57852-3 Hardback
ISBN 978-1-009-35068-6 Paperback
ISSN 2754-6144 (online)
ISSN 2754-6136 (print)

Cambridge University Press & Assessment has no responsibility for the persistence or accuracy of URLs for external or third-party internet websites referred to in this publication and does not guarantee that any content on such websites is, or will remain, accurate or appropriate.

Mass Polarization across Time and Space

Elements in Comparative Political Behavior

DOI: 10.1017/9781009350662
First published online: February 2025

Isaac D. Mehlhaff
The University of Chicago

Author for correspondence: Isaac D. Mehlhaff, imehlhaff@uchicago.edu

Abstract: Mass polarization is one of the defining features of politics in the twenty-first century, but efforts to understand its causes and effects are often hindered by empirical challenges related to measurement and data availability. To address these challenges and provide a common standard of analysis for researchers, this Element presents the Polarization in Comparative Attitudes Project (PolarCAP). PolarCAP clearly defines polarization as a property of group relations and uses a Bayesian measurement model to estimate smooth panels of ideological and affective polarization across ninety-two countries and forty-nine years. The author uses these data to provide a descriptive account of mass polarization across time and space. They further show how PolarCAP facilitates substantive inference by applying it to three sets of variables often hypothesized as causes or consequences of polarization: institutional design, economic crisis, and democracy. Open-source software makes PolarCAP easily accessible to scholars and practitioners.

Keywords: polarization, mass politics, public opinion, latent variables, measurement, democracy, institutions, political economy, affect, ideology

© Isaac D. Mehlhaff 2025

ISBNs: 9781009578523 (HB), 9781009350686 (PB), 9781009350662 (OC)
ISSNs: 2754-6144 (online), 2754-6136 (print)

Contents

1 Mass Polarization in Comparative Politics: Concepts and Challenges 1

2 Estimating Country-Year Panels of Mass Polarization 13

3 Polarization across Time and Space: Descriptive Analyses 36

4 Correlates of Mass Polarization 53

5 Advancing the Scientific Study of Polarization 67

   References 75

1 Mass Polarization in Comparative Politics: Concepts and Challenges

Political polarization has long been a key concept in comparative politics. Scholars have highlighted its connection to a wide range of important political phenomena, such as democracy (Linz, 1978), representation (Bornschier, 2019), party system dynamics (Sartori, 1976), and economic crisis (Hobolt & Tilley, 2016). My focus here is mass polarization – the division of public opinion and political society into tightly knit, highly differentiated groups of partisans or ideological adherents.

Mass polarization affects some of the most critical aspects of political life. It is associated with lower government spending (Lindqvist & Östling, 2010), it can lead to increased support for extreme parties (Ezrow et al., 2014), and it may even contribute to political instability and repression in developing areas (Bratton & van deWalle, 1997). The potential drivers and mitigators of mass polarization are no less consequential. It appears to be exacerbated by economic inequality and disproportionate representation in legislative institutions (Matakos et al., 2016; Pontusson & Rueda, 2008), but may be ameliorated by increasing the descriptive representation of historically underrepresented groups (Adams et al., 2023).

This real-world import has sparked a rapid proliferation of research using a comparative perspective to understand the causes and consequences of mass polarization. Gidron et al.'s (2020) recent effort to characterize mass affective polarization around the world immediately garnered much scholarly interest. Their study of affective polarization across two decades and twenty Western publics showed how it varies across country context and correlates with economic and institutional variables, a line of inquiry they continued to advance in subsequent years (e.g. Adams et al., 2023; Gidron et al., 2023; Horne et al., 2023). Many other scholars have built on this work and offered their own accounts of comparative polarization (see, among many others, Algara & Zur, 2023; Reiljan et al., 2024; Wagner, 2021).

Although this research agenda has advanced empirically grounded explanations of where polarization comes from and how it affects polities, it has also been beset by challenges that constrain the inferences scholars can draw. Appropriate cross-national survey data are scarce, analyses of what little data do exist often fail to marry theory to practice, and measurement in multiparty systems is frequently problematic. Measurement concerns and lack of spatio-temporal variation undermine scholars' ability to answer substantive questions and draw generalizable conclusions.

This Element charts a path to overcome these challenges. I present the Polarization in Comparative Attitudes Project (PolarCAP), which provides a common standard of analysis for researchers by clearly defining and measuring polarization and estimating smooth panels of mass polarization across time and space. I use the resulting data to provide both descriptive and explanatory accounts of mass polarization in comparative politics.

1.1 A Group-Based Conceptualization of Polarization

Measures developed with insufficient attention to the concepts they are designed to tap run the risk of producing misleading evidence. Before I can tackle the problems surrounding the measurement of mass polarization, it is important to be clear about what concept I aim to estimate. Unfortunately, there is no one definition of polarization around which scholars have rallied, and this disagreement on theoretical concept likely contributes to disagreement on when and where polarization is occurring (Hetherington, 2009).

I provide a minimal definition that posits polarization as a property of group relations. Polarization is a phenomenon that happens both between and within groups, emerging when group members disagree with members of other groups and agree with members of their own. Mehlhaff (2024) shows how this understanding of polarization translates into two conceptual features: distance from opponents (intergroup heterogeneity) and concentration within groups (intragroup homogeneity). Theories of polarization frequently reference both features, if only implicitly (DiMaggio et al., 1996; Esteban & Ray, 1994; Fortunato & Stevenson, 2021; McCoy et al., 2018; Traber et al., 2023).

Disagreement or distance between groups – intergroup heterogeneity – is one critical feature of polarization. For instance, as parties' ideal points gradually approach opposite ends of a policy space, that party system becomes more polarized (Sartori, 1976). Compromise becomes exceedingly difficult when partisans' median issue preferences are far apart, not only because partisans are more inclined to dislike their opponents (Iyengar et al., 2012; Reiljan, 2020), but because their preferences are so different that at least one group would view any middle ground as an unacceptable capitulation (Persily, 2015). One consequence of an unwillingness to work together is legislative gridlock and ineffective government (Binder, 1999), which might itself contribute to further resentment and conflict among citizens who identify with different parties or belong to different socioeconomic strata.[1] When parties are farther apart

---

[1] Sigelman and Yough (1978) discuss the theoretical importance of socioeconomic linkages in political polarization.

ideologically, they are also more likely to contribute to declining comity by airing negative campaign advertisements or coarsening the language with which they discuss politics (Ansolabehere & Iyengar, 1995; Mason, 2018).

Intergroup heterogeneity is often the main conceptual feature with which scholars of polarization engage. However, the degree to which groups are tightly concentrated – intragroup homogeneity – is also important. At a basic level, intragroup homogeneity can make groups more distinct; as the ideal points of party members cluster more tightly together, each party becomes more internally homogeneous, parties share less in common with each other, and the party system becomes more polarized. Crucially, polarization can increase in this manner even in the *absence* of increasing intergroup heterogeneity. Party sorting is one process through which this happens; individuals do not become more extreme but the population nevertheless polarizes due to individuals sorting themselves into parties with positions similar to their own (Levendusky, 2009). Conversely, parties may themselves be internally fractured (Groenendyk et al., 2020). It is important to account for such divisions within parties (low intragroup homogeneity) because they decrease the extent to which parties can act as cohesive units and provide an opportunity for individuals to defect to another party.

Even more important than the mechanical connection between intragroup homogeneity and polarization is the theoretical importance of this feature for understanding group conflict. Individuals tend to accurately perceive increases in the homogeneity of their in-group (Park & Judd, 1990). Greater in-group homogeneity, in turn, strengthens group identity and can lead to greater intergroup conflict, including among networks of political partisans (Huddy, 2001; Parsons, 2015). Similarly, individuals typically overestimate the homogeneity of out-groups, these assessments become even more exaggerated as the out-group becomes more homogeneous (Guinote & Fiske, 2003), and the result is often heightened bias against the out-group (Tajfel, 1982; Wilder, 1978). For example, when partisans misperceive other parties as being mostly comprised of negatively valanced constituent groups, they tend to see those out-partisans as more extreme, view them negatively, and express stronger allegiance to their own party (Ahler & Sood, 2018). In sum, group perceptions shape intergroup relations (Xiao et al., 2016).

The prominent debate on whether polarization exists in the American mass public illustrates the importance of explicitly theorizing and incorporating both features into theories and measures of polarization. In the early twenty-first century, the United States experienced increases in both intergroup heterogeneity and intragroup homogeneity. Indeed, Fiorina (2005) conceded the parties had become farther apart, but dismissed this change as unimportant for polarization because the increase in distance between party means mostly resulted from party sorting, not increasing extremity.

In their critique of Fiorina (2005), Abramowitz and Saunders (2008) theorized polarization in terms of distance between parties (intergroup heterogeneity). Yet their most compelling evidence of polarization actually revealed increasing intragroup homogeneity. Specifically, they found Republicans were increasingly likely to adopt conservative positions on a wide range of issues, while Democrats were increasingly likely to take liberal positions on those same issues. This increase in what Converse (1964) labeled "issue constraint" reflects changing opinion patterns *within* parties, not between them. With the United States becoming qualitatively more polarized over the past twenty-five years, it is noteworthy that the foundational evidence from this debate better reflects the importance of intragroup homogeneity, even as the dialogue focused on the distance between parties. Incorporating both features allows scholars to paint a more complete portrait of American polarization, depicting both the degree of separation between parties and the degree of similarity within them.

Polarization can manifest in a variety of ways, from the party system (Dalton, 2008), to legislative institutions (Singer, 2016), and even the political geography of citizens' environments (Nall, 2018). I am concerned with ideological and affective polarization in the mass public, the definitions and measures of which follow from the group-based concept I describe previously. An ideologically polarized political society is characterized by two or more distinct groups that cluster tightly around their ideal points and share little in common with each other ideologically. These groups take the form of political parties in this case, but one could also apply this concept to groups defined on the basis of race, income, or other delimiters. Similarly, affective polarization is characterized by citizens grouping together based on their political party or coalition, with these individuals holding similar, highly favorable attitudes toward their own partisan group and similar, highly unfavorable attitudes toward other partisan groups.

1.2 From Concept to Empirics

The most commonly used (and most abundant) sources of data capturing citizens' political ideology and party affect are public opinion surveys. In fact, surveys in different countries and in different time periods use similar items quite often; soliciting self-placement on the left-right scale, for example, has been a mainstay on public opinion surveys for nearly forty years.

I use two types of survey items. To capture political ideology, I use left-right self-placement (Iversen and Soskice, 2015; Jensen & Thomsen, 2013; Lelkes, 2016).[2] Although multi-item batteries of policy positions might be preferable for measuring ideology, constraints on data availability and computational resources make left-right self-placements a practical alternative. These items reflect citizens' positions on a wide variety of issues (Zechmeister & Corral, 2013) and analyses of party manifestos suggest that the unidimensional structure of ideology implicit in left-right self-placement closely approximates party competition in most democracies (McDonald et al., 2007).

To capture party affect, I use partisan feeling thermometers, a popular survey item among scholars studying affective polarization in comparative contexts (Reiljan, 2020; Wagner, 2021; Ward & Tavits, 2019).[3] Gidron et al. (2022) validate feeling thermometers as a measure of party affect. Specifically, they show feeling thermometers capture sentiment toward party supporters and correlate with other measures of affective polarization, such as social distance and discrimination in economic games.

Because left-right self-placement and feeling thermometer items are asked consistently across survey programs and time periods, they offer an intriguing opportunity to investigate mass polarization across space and time. As a first step, I collate data from a wide range of nationally representative public opinion surveys that ask left-right self-placement or party feeling thermometer items. This effort yields approximately 3.5 million individual observations across thirty-five different survey programs. Tables 1 and 2 display the survey programs, how many country-years each contributes, and the range of dates covered by each.

Although this collection likely represents the largest aggregation of such public opinion data to date, its structure makes it difficult to use. Each survey is a snapshot of public opinion at the time the survey was conducted. Simply calculating an estimate of polarization in each country-year would produce observations scattered across time and space, leaving large gaps in the time series and only providing information on some countries at a handful of time points.

The data fragmentation can be seen graphically in Figure 1. It plots each year for which survey data is available in four exemplar countries, to which I return in Section 3: Mexico, South Africa, Spain, and the United States. Open

---

[2] Some surveys ask about closely related concepts, such as "liberal" and "conservative." I include these types of ideological placements as well.
[3] I exclude items asking about feelings toward political leaders, as these may tap into a different attitude (Reiljan et al., 2024).

Table 1 Survey programs and coverage (political ideology)

Survey Program	Country-Years	Year Range
AmericasBarometer	112	2004–2019
Australian Election Study	7	1987–2016
Parliamentary Election Belarus[4]	2	1995–2002
Canadian Election Study	2	1988–1993
Comparative National Election Project	24	1992–2018
Croatian National Election Study	5	1990–2003
Comparative Study of Electoral Systems	176	1996–2018
Party Preferences Czech Republic	1	2000
Eurobarometer	726	1973–2019
Central and Eastern Eurobarometer[5]	56	1990–2004
European Values Study	59	1981–2019
Hungarian Election Study	1	1994
Icelandic National Election Study	4	1987–2016
Israel National Election Study	9	1981–2016
Latinobarómetro	238	1995–2018
Statistics Norway Election Survey	2	1989–2017
New Zealand Election Study	5	1990–2017
Pew Global Attitudes	19	2002–2018
Election Study Serbia[6]	3	1990–2002
Slovenian Public Opinion Survey	1	1997
Statistics Sweden Election Study	3	1988–1994
Swiss Election Study	8	1971–2019
American National Election Studies	12	1972–2002
General Social Survey	1	2014
World Values Survey	177	1981–2016

circles indicate years for which data on political ideology are available and closed circles indicate years for which data on both ideology and party affect are available.[7]

Some cases, such as Spain, have excellent coverage, with ideological data available for every year beginning in 1985. In other cases, data are sparse.

---

[4] Includes *Democratic Attitudes in Belarus*.
[5] Includes *Consolidation of Democracy in Central and Eastern Europe and Candidate Countries Eurobarometer*.
[6] Includes *Political and Social Attitudes in Serbia*.
[7] There are no country-years for which only party affect data is available.

Table 2 Survey programs and coverage (party affect)

Survey Program	Country-Years	Year Range
Australian Election Study	2	1993–2016
Canadian Election Study	3	1988–2000
Comparative National Election Project	25	1992–2018
Croatian National Election Study	2	2000–2003
Comparative Study of Electoral Systems	178	1996–2018
Danish Election Study	3	1994–2011
Politbarometer	37	1977–2018
Hungarian Election Study	1	1994
Icelandic National Election Study	5	1987–2017
Israel National Election Study	7	1988–2019
Dutch Parliamentary Election Study	3	1986–2012
Statistics Norway Election Survey	2	1989–2017
New Zealand Election Study	5	1990–2017
Polish National Election Study	1	2000
Current Problems of Slovakia	1	1999
Slovenian Public Opinion Survey	1	1997
Statistics Sweden Election Study	4	1988–2010
Swiss Election Study	2	1975–1995
British Election Study	3	1992–2010
American National Election Studies	14	1978–2016

South Africa has only twelve total years of ideological data available over the half-century under investigation. Party affect data is even less consistent. Indeed, party affect data is never available for all four cases in the same year. Inconsistent data availability has consequences for the types of substantive conclusions one can draw about mass polarization. Rather than a fragmented time series, scholars need country-year *panels* of aggregate opinion, with smooth time series estimates in a large number of countries across a broad swath of time.

In addition, cross-national survey research imposes an additional set of problems: Item wording and response options often differ slightly from year to year or from country to country. Even when they are identical, they may be interpreted differently depending on context (Ariely & Davidov, 2012; Stegmueller, 2011). Different surveys in different years sometimes use a different number of response categories to the same item. Different survey

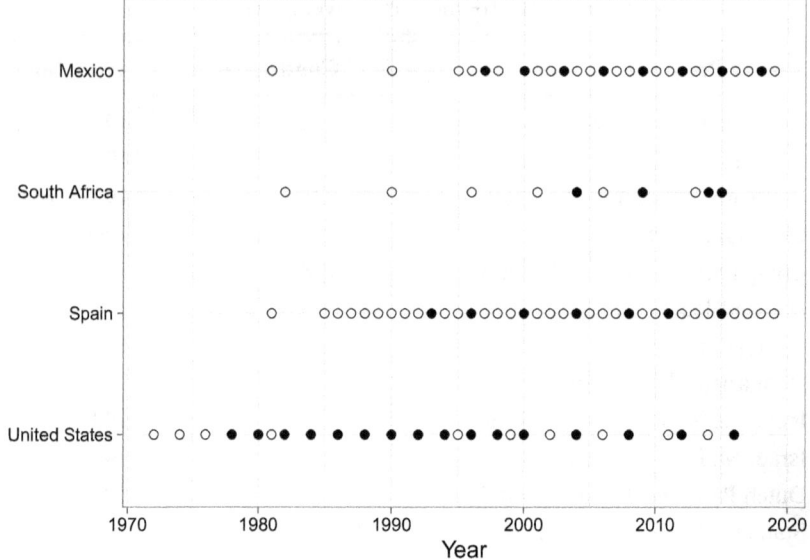

Figure 1 Data sparsity in four exemplar countries

vendors use different sampling procedures. To produce country-year panels of polarization estimates, I must correct for these non-stochastic sources of variation. I construct a model to do so in Section 2.

First, however, I need to describe how I prepare the raw survey responses for analysis. To illustrate these data preparation procedures and how the output of the following measurement model translates raw data into polarization estimates, I use the United States in 2016 – the final presidential election year covered by my data collection – as a running example throughout this section and the next. I choose the United States from among the exemplar countries in Figure 1 because its two-party system facilitates a simpler, more visually straightforward explanation, but the same intuition applies to all cases.

First, following Boxell et al. (2024), I apply an affine transformation to each survey's responses to ensure they all have support on the same interval – $[0, 10]$ for ideology and $[0, 100]$ for party affect.[8] Second, I calculate the

---

[8] This requires me to assume cardinality in the response options, an assumption routinely employed by scholars calculating statistics such as mean or standard deviation from these types of data. I can partially relax this assumption later by constructing a latent variable model that operates on categories instead of values.

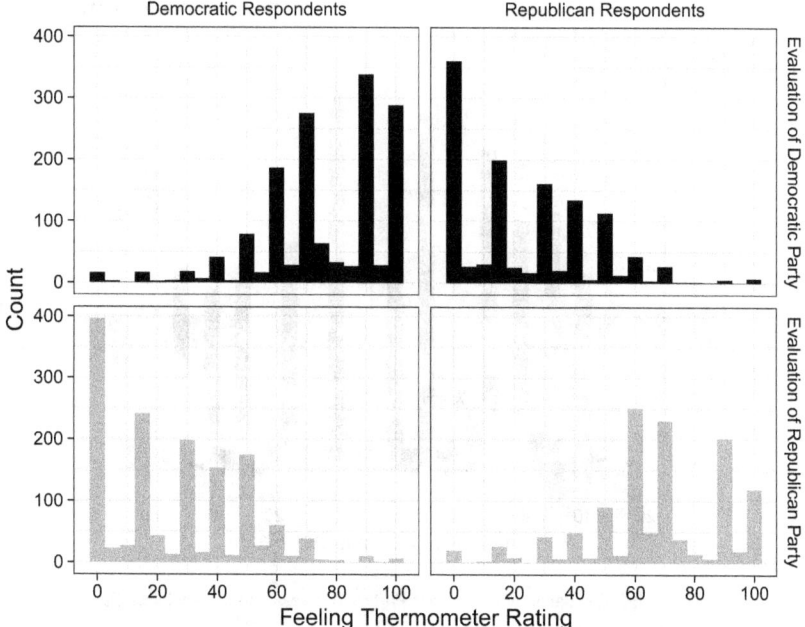

Figure 2 US running example: Weighted feeling thermometer response counts, disaggregated by party and target of evaluation

number of respondents offering each response option, weighted to be nationally representative using weights provided by the survey program.[9]

Figure 2 displays histograms of these weighted response counts for the feeling thermometer item in the United States, broken down by both the respondents' party and the party they are evaluating.[10] The upper-left facet therefore shows Democrats' evaluations of the Democratic Party while the lower-left facet shows their evaluations of the Republican Party. The facets on the right show analogous responses for Republicans. These data reflect what one might expect from Americans' feelings toward the parties: Democrats feel warmly toward the Democratic Party and coldly toward the Republican Party, indicated by the left- and right-skewed distributions in the upper- and lower-left facets, respectively. The opposite is true for Republicans.

Unlike many other scholars measuring affective polarization (e.g. Adams et al., 2023; Gidron et al., 2023; Reiljan et al., 2024), however, I am not interested in these dyadic assessments, where party members evaluate each party in

---

[9] The unweighted distribution appears nearly identical to the weighted distribution in this case, so I do not show it here.

[10] I focus on only Democratic and Republican respondents to simplify the visualization, but the final data contains all respondents regardless of party identification.

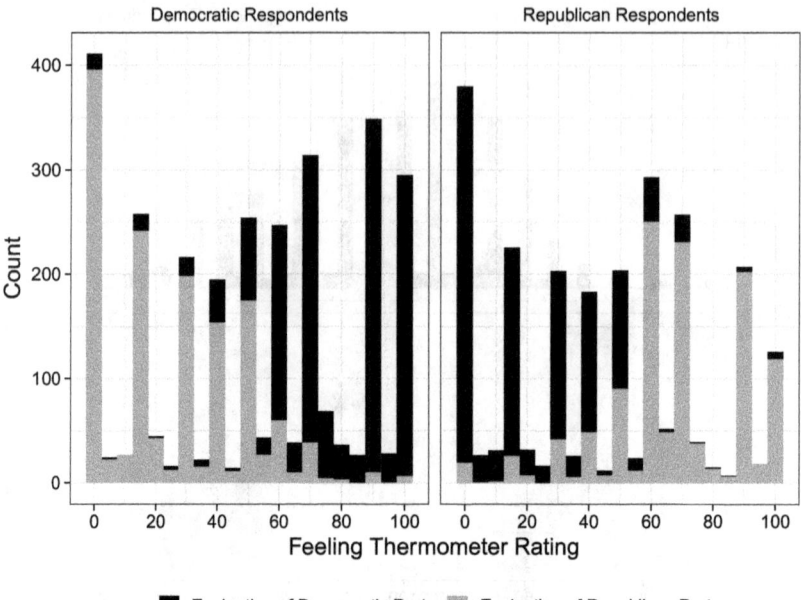

Figure 3 US running example: Weighted feeling thermometer response counts, disaggregated by party

turn. As I discuss in Section 2, the complexity of party identity in multi-party systems makes evaluations of a single in-party against all others a rather unnatural window into political sentiment (Wagner, 2021). Instead, the macro-level understanding of polarization I previously described requires a *distribution* of opinion which, in the United States, is likely to be bimodal.

Figure 3 therefore shows how I recover this bimodal distribution by simply collapsing the two feeling thermometer items into one unidimensional scale. Just as in Figure 2, the black portions of the histogram bars represent evaluations of the Democratic Party and the gray portions represent evaluations of the Republican Party. Instead of two unimodal, oppositely skewed distributions for Democratic and Republican respondents, I now have a single bimodal distribution for the members of each party.

Further aggregating responses among all partisan identifications produces the distribution in Figure 4. This plot shows the full distribution of weighted response counts to the feeling thermometer items. The bimodal nature of this distribution is still evident, and it is the polarization of this distribution in which I am interested. In some ways, this departs from how many scholars have approached the quantitative study of polarization. My focus on aggregate distributions extends directly from my definition of polarization as a macro-level phenomenon. A clear connection between concept and operationalization

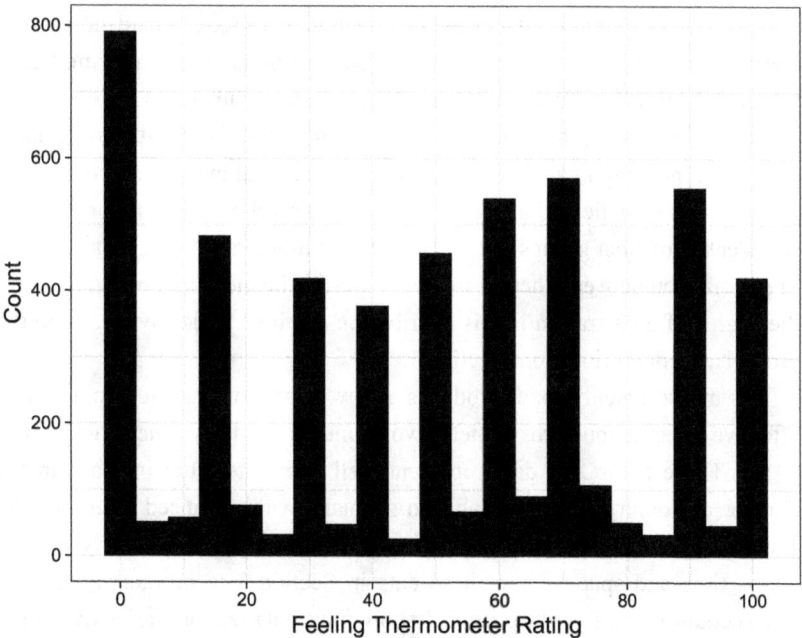

Figure 4 US running example: Full distribution of weighted feeling thermometer response counts

is an important pillar of social science; in Section 2, I expand further on how I pursue this connection.

I focus on the feeling thermometer data in this running example because it is more complex and requires more detailed explanation, but the same intuition applies to the left-right self-placement data. The key difference is that the latter is already on a unidimensional scale, so simply plotting the original, weighted data produces a plot much like the one in Figure 4. These weighted counts are my starting point for the measurement model in Section 2.

1.3 Road Map

In this section, I defined polarization as a group-based concept, a phenomenon that occurs both between and within groups. It possesses two conceptual features: distance from opponents (intergroup heterogeneity) and concentration within groups (intragroup homogeneity). Accounting for both features is a fundamental aspect of my approach to measuring and studying mass polarization. I further described the data sources I draw on to estimate mass polarization according to this definition. The remainder of the Element describes the Polarization in Comparative Attitudes Project (PolarCAP) and demonstrates its utility.

In Section 2, I explicate the measurement model I use to estimate mass polarization by country-year. This model extends existing latent variable models to preserve the full distribution of latent opinion – not just an ideal point estimate – while still accounting for sources of non-stochastic variation. It also smooths over time, meaning I can estimate mass polarization at every time point, even if no surveys were fielded in a given country-year. I show how mixture models can identify distinct groups in the latent distribution, facilitating measurement of polarization between them. Finally, I describe the measure I use to quantify the degree of polarization in this distribution and how it displays fealty to the group-based definition from Section 1.

This measurement model produces a new dataset of mass ideological and affective polarization across ninety-two countries and forty-nine years (1971–2019). These PolarCAP data represent well over a ten-fold increase in the number of country-years available to scholars, with enhanced temporal and geographic coverage. To illustrate how PolarCAP enables scholarly inquiry across time and space, I use these data in Section 3 to produce a descriptive account of mass polarization. I show how polarization varies over time within four exemplar countries – Mexico, South Africa, Spain, and the United States – and across countries at two temporal cross-sections. This exercise also helps demonstrate the construct validity of PolarCAP. In each case, PolarCAP estimates match important social and political events, suggesting that the measurement model in Section 2 produces sensible estimates.

In Section 4, I apply PolarCAP to three sets of variables often theorized as causes or consequences of polarization: political institutions, economic indicators, and democracy. The thinness of available data and the frequent incongruence between concept and measure in polarization scholarship often makes it difficult to assess how polarization relates to these critical topics. The structure of PolarCAP, however, is well-suited to facilitate substantive inference. Results suggest that mass polarization varies with institutional design and is associated with democratic backsliding, but theories that claim polarization results from economic circumstances do not appear to generalize outside the United States.

In Section 5, I reflect on the state of mass polarization research, providing a non-exhaustive outline of areas in which scholars have made progress, areas in which we still have much to learn, and how researchers might leverage PolarCAP to help answer unresolved questions or even revisit questions we previously thought to be answered. For example, do certain institutional configurations interrupt the association between polarization and democratic backsliding? Does polarization increase political participation? Scholars have broached many such questions in studies focusing on a single case or limited cross-sections, but the broadly cross-national, time-series nature of PolarCAP enables scholars to gain explanatory – even causal – purchase that has not previously been possible.

Researchers may freely access PolarCAP estimates and their associated standard errors through an open-source R package – PolarCAP: Access the Polarization in Comparative Attitudes Project. This package is available on the Comprehensive R Archive Network and includes helper functions for retrieving and manipulating the data (Mehlhaff, 2023). PolarCAP's companion website provides short vignettes explaining how to incorporate the package into common data analysis pipelines, and it also provides the full dataset in several formats for those working in other computing environments (https://imehlhaff.net/PolarCAP).

2 Estimating Country-Year Panels of Mass Polarization

In the previous section, I conceptualized polarization as a property of group dynamics and showed that appropriate cross-national survey data are scarce. A clear concept is of little help in answering substantive questions if data are few and far between. In this section, I therefore turn my attention to this problem of data scarcity. Complicating matters further, the raw survey data I described in Section 1 present formidable challenges. Question wording and response options sometimes differ across contexts. Different survey vendors use different sampling procedures. And, most critically, many countries were polled irregularly, resulting in frequently interrupted time series.

I build a Bayesian measurement model to overcome these challenges. My primary objective in fitting this measurement model is approximating a population-level distribution of ideology and party affect for each country-year. A secondary objective is to collate the vast collection of aggregate, country-level survey data available to scholars and correct for non-stochastic variation arising as a consequence of these data being splintered across time, space, and survey programs.

The result of the Polarization in Comparative Attitudes Project (PolarCAP) is a new dataset consisting of 4,508 country-year estimates of ideological polarization and 2,340 country-year estimates of affective polarization, spread across ninety-two countries and forty-nine years. Compared to existing data sets of mass polarization (e.g. Boxell et al., 2024; Gidron et al., 2020; Wagner, 2021), PolarCAP boasts well over a tenfold increase in the number of country-years available to scholars, with substantially enhanced temporal and geographic breadth.

2.1 Objectives

Given the conceptualization of polarization and the unique set of challenges imposed by the survey data described in Section 1, I identify five attributes that a measurement model of polarization must possess. First, it should treat polarization as a latent property of aggregate public opinion – a property of which we gain only small glimpses through random samples of individual survey responses. This model should thus estimate aggregate public opinion at the country-year level.

Second, the model should extend beyond more traditional item response models (e.g. Reckase, 2009; Wirth & Edwards, 2007) to smooth not only across survey items, but also to smooth over time, resulting in country-level public opinion panels with no gaps in the time series. This characteristic is critical not only for descriptive accuracy, but also for using the resulting dataset for theory testing.

Third, the model should preserve the integrity of observed, discrete survey responses, modeling the number of responses given to a response option rather than some other derived quantity (Caughey et al., 2019; Caughey & Warshaw, 2015; Linzer, 2013). Scholars often collapse multinomial or ordinal response options into a binary scale or model a post-processed quantity such as the proportion of respondents giving each response option. The consequence of these practices is to throw away information about respondents who fall into extreme categories (Abramowitz & Saunders, 2008) – a key quantity of interest in the measurement of polarization. Directly modeling the number of responses confers the additional benefit of incorporating sampling error.

Fourth, the model should adjust the link between observed survey responses and unobserved latent opinion by correcting for non-stochastic sources of variation. This is especially critical in models of polarization. Failing to correct for variation in item discrimination leads to spurious estimates of polarization (Hill & Tausanovitch, 2015), and failing to account for differential item functioning – a key concern in comparative public opinion (Ariely & Davidov, 2012; Stegmueller, 2011) – leads to underestimates of polarization in ideological self-placement (Hare et al., 2015).

Finally, the model should preserve, adjust, and estimate a *distribution* of opinion in each country-year, rather than a single point. Final polarization estimates can then be recovered from these country-year distributions. Polarization is a group-based phenomenon that implies both intergroup heterogeneity and intragroup homogeneity. Similar measurement models focus on estimating ideal points (e.g. Caughey et al., 2019; Claassen, 2019), but measuring polarization requires knowledge of the full, potentially multimodal distribution of latent attitudes – not just the overall mean.

2.2 Approaches to Modeling Dynamic Public Opinion

The type of aggregate-level, time-smoothing latent variable model required for this task has been the subject of considerable research in social scientific methodology. Beck's (1989) measurement model with Kalman filtering and Stimson's (1991, 2018) dyad-ratios algorithm were two foundational approaches to smoothing aggregate opinion over time. Beck presented a maximum-likelihood approach to combining multiple survey items into one estimate of presidential approval, while accounting for measurement error. He then used a Kalman filter to smooth those estimates over time. Soon after, Stimson developed his dyad-ratios algorithm to estimate policy mood in the American mass public. His key insight was that although different survey items reveal different levels of policy support, over-time *changes* in those levels of support across items can be used to estimate smooth time series of policy mood. Both approaches advanced research on dynamic public opinion and have been used in a wide range of substantive studies (Carlin et al., 2015; Erikson et al., 2002; Green & Jennings, 2012).

The proliferation of Bayesian methods in the early 2000s quickened progress in this area. Jackman (2005) provided a basic formulation of this type of model, with an application to vote intention across an Australian campaign season. Jackman's model corrected for "house effects" – bias introduced by variation in polling methodology across survey programs – and smoothed over time with a "random walk," a simple procedure that models each time period's level of voter support as a noisy function of voter support in the previous time period. Voeten and Brewer (2006) went a step further, incorporating item bias effects that allow them to combine different survey items. Each of these approaches focused on estimating aggregate opinion in a single country.

To make generalizable inferences about polarization's causes and effects, however, scholars should leverage global survey programs. Employing a dynamic group-level IRT model, Caughey and Warshaw (2015) took a step toward estimating cross-national opinion, but their model is most useful for estimating opinion within small groups, such as gender or racial categories, for which the researcher may not have representative samples.[11] Claassen (2019) provided a more general Bayesian framework for estimating country-year

---

[11] See also Caughey et al. (2019).

opinion, with the added bonus of enhanced computational efficiency, and Tai et al. (2024) offer a method for incorporating measurement uncertainty. The progress made in dynamic aggregate opinion modeling has been substantial. But these models are primarily concerned with estimating ideal points – a single data point for each country-year to summarize policy mood, democratic support, or executive approval.

For calculating polarization, then, existing models will not suffice. Such measurement requires a model that estimates a *distribution* of latent public opinion. Some authors take a step in this direction by directly estimating the standard deviation of the ideal point estimates and treating these standard deviations as measures of polarization (e.g. Solt, 2020b). As I explain later, however, that approach is problematic because the dispersion of a population-level parameter does not fully capture a group-based concept like polarization.

The measurement model I present incorporates two key innovations to allow for the calculation of cross-national polarization estimates that correct for sources of unobserved heterogeneity, smooth over time, and conform to the group-based understanding of polarization. First, I extend existing approaches to model discrete data, thereby preserving the full distribution of opinion instead of reducing each country-year to a single data point. Second, I employ a mixture model – a model capable of representing subgroups in a population – to generate two pieces of information that correspond neatly to the two features of polarization: the ideal point of each group in the latent space (corresponding to intergroup heterogeneity) and the standard deviation of each group's distribution (corresponding to intragroup homogeneity).

2.3 Adjusting Distributions for Non-Stochastic Variation: A Dynamic Latent Variable Model

The next two subsections explicate the model I use to estimate smooth panels of mass polarization, keeping in mind the five requirements I identified previously. Throughout, I use bold Latin letters to indicate vectors of data (e.g. **y**), bold Greek letters to indicate vectors of parameters (e.g. $\boldsymbol{\theta}$), and non-bold characters to denote scalar quantities of each (e.g. y, θ). In the case of scalar quantities, uppercase letters signify the total number of the given quantity, while lowercase letters denote individual categories of the same (e.g. $k \in \{1, \ldots, K\}$). For clarity of exposition, I omit some non-essential information from the main text but briefly address these omissions in technical footnotes, which are clearly identified as such. These technical notes are intended for mathematically inclined or especially interested readers and can be safely ignored by those desiring a more general understanding of the model.

I begin with a dynamic latent variable model similar to the one Claassen (2019) developed to estimate ideal points from binary survey responses. As mentioned previously, I aim to preserve the discrete structure of survey data. I therefore model a vector $\mathbf{y}_{itj}$ of length K, which contains the number of respondents in country i at time t who offer response option k to survey item j:

$$\mathbf{y}_{itj} \sim \text{Multinom}(N_{itj}, \boldsymbol{\pi}_{itj}), \tag{1}$$

where N_{itj} is a scalar representing the number of observations collected for a survey item in a given country-year – weighted to be nationally representative where necessary – and $\boldsymbol{\pi}_{itj}$ is a vector of probabilities for that item's response categories. Countries i, years t, and response options k are self-explanatory in this context, but distinctions between survey items j may be less so. One of the key benefits of latent variable models is that they account for variation introduced by different types of survey items, so I need to identify each unique type of item. For example, some use a "liberal-conservative" scale to capture self-reported ideology, while others use "left-right." Even within survey items, varying sampling techniques across survey programs may result in different response distributions. These sources of variation – item type and survey program – are captured by j.

Similar to how one might use a multinomial logit to model categorical or ordinal data in a linear model, this part of the model takes the total number of observations N_{itj} and uses the observed response counts $\mathbf{y}_{itj}$ to estimate the probability that a response falls into each response category, keeping country-years and survey items separate from each other. Just like $\mathbf{y}_{itj}$, $\boldsymbol{\pi}_{itj}$ is therefore also of length K, as the values of the two vectors are directly related.

This multinomial specification builds on an important insight by Goplerud (2019): Survey items with multiple response categories, though typically treated as binary or ordinal by ideal point models, can be modeled as a series of separate response options. Doing so allows each response option to take its own set of latent parameters and to be adjusted separately for item bias effects, country-year latent effects, and the like.

To take a hypothetical example, imagine that respondents interpret the meaning of response options on a "liberal-conservative" scale differently than they would on a "left-right" scale, such that soliciting self-reported ideology on the former makes respondents more likely to select the extreme categories on the scale. This is clearly a source of variation for which one would want to account, as it has direct implications for polarization estimates. However, this variation would be averaged out in standard latent variable models – perhaps a desirable property when estimating ideal points, but not when estimating polarization. To fully correct for statistical artifacts stemming from the data-generating process, the model must be able to adjust each response category, not just the overall average. The multinomial specification in (1) allows the model to accomplish this important task.

I now dig deeper into how the model handles these and other sources of variation. The survey data I employ provide noisy signals of aggregate public opinion and approximate – but do not capture directly – ideology or party affect in a given population. Instead, my goal is to use these survey data to recover estimates of latent country-year ideology or party affect, which I denote as the vector θ_{it}, of length K. The first step in incorporating this country-year parameter is to place a Dirichlet prior on π_{itj}. A Dirichlet distribution takes a vector of positive real numbers – α_{itj} in (2) – and transforms it into a vector of the same length with values that sum to one. This makes it a useful distribution to model my response probabilities π_{itj}.

I could simply model π_{itj} directly as a function of latent traits, but adding the Dirichlet prior allows for additional dispersion in survey responses beyond sampling error. This additional error covers variation introduced by things like interviewer ethnicity or survey mode (Adida et al., 2016; Weisberg, 2005) – factors that are often unobserved but nevertheless can influence the survey responses interviewees are willing to give. To the extent that the following latent variable model does not correct for all sources of non-stochastic variation, I can rely on the Dirichlet prior to absorb additional error. Formally,

$$\pi_{itj} \sim \text{Dir}(\alpha_{itj}), \qquad (2)$$

where α_{itj} is a vector of concentration parameters $\alpha_{itj1}, \ldots, \alpha_{itjK}$. The α_{itj} parameters in the Dirichlet distribution can be thought of as corresponding to the π_{itj} parameters in the multinomial distribution in (1), such that a higher concentration parameter α_{itjk} indicates that response option k is more likely, and therefore carries a higher probability π_{itjk}. These concentration parameters are difficult to work with, however, so I reparameterize this Dirichlet prior to take a vector of expectation parameters η_{itj} – which can more easily be represented as the outcome of a latent variable model – and scale parameter ϕ:

$$\eta_{itj} = \frac{\alpha_{itj}}{\sum_{k=1}^{K} \alpha_{itjk}},$$

$$\phi = \sum_{k=1}^{K} \alpha_{itjk}, \qquad (3)$$

$$\rightarrow \alpha_{itj} = \eta_{itj}\phi,$$

where $\phi \sim \Gamma(4, 0.1)$ and η_{itj} is modeled as a function of latent traits.

It is here that the model adjusts latent estimates by correcting for various sources of bias. In particular, the model incorporates item bias effects λ_j, item-country latent effects δ_{ij}, and my primary quantity of interest, country-year latent effects θ_{it}. The former two values are scalars while the latter is a vector of length K:[12]

$$\eta_{itj} = \text{softmax}(\lambda_j + \delta_{ij} + \theta_{it}). \tag{4}$$

Each of these parameters corrects for important sources of variation. First, minor differences in the wording of survey questions or response options might impact how they are understood by respondents and, consequently, the response options chosen by those respondents. For example, asking respondents to place themselves on a "liberal-conservative" scale may lead respondents to think of themselves as more extreme – and therefore to place themselves closer to the scale endpoints – than if the survey asked respondents to place themselves on a "left-right" scale, which might evoke a slightly different understanding of ideology. Or perhaps one survey provides a short description of what "left-right" means in the context of politics, while other surveys do not (Yeung & Quek, forthcoming). The item bias effects λ_j adjust the latent estimates for these possibilities, ensuring that the polarization estimates I eventually get from the model do not reflect these undesirable sources of variation.

Second, survey items may be understood differently from one country to the next. This is a common problem in comparative survey research known as differential item functioning or lack of equivalence (Stegmueller, 2011). Citizens in countries with greater degrees of party system fragmentation, for instance, may have a poorer understanding of the left-right scale and where they stand on it, relative to citizens in countries with fewer parties (Zechmeister & Corral, 2013). I do not want this sort of variation to artificially inflate or deflate polarization estimates, so I include item-country latent effects δ_{ij} to help adjust the latent estimates accordingly.

Other authors have dealt with this source of variation differently. Gidron et al. (2020) and Lelkes and Westwood (2017) argue that taking the difference between in- and out-party feeling thermometers ameliorates bias from differential item functioning in estimates of affective polarization. There are two drawbacks to employing this strategy. First, making such a claim requires the assumption that the degree of bias is uniform across parties within countries. For example, if in-party feeling thermometer evaluations are five degrees

---

[12] Technical note: (4) is implemented as $\eta_{itj} = \text{softmax}((\lambda_j + \delta_{ij})\mathbf{e} + \theta_{it})$, where $\mathbf{e}$ is an all-ones vector of length K.

higher in one country compared to others, the out-party feeling thermometer evaluations in that country must also be five degrees higher. If the magnitude or sign of that discrepancy is different from one party to the next, the difference between them will still carry bias from differential item functioning. Second, the differencing approach would not work for estimates of ideological polarization, which are captured with a single survey item. Modeling the country-item bias directly, as I do here, requires weaker assumptions and is more flexible.

Readers familiar with item-response theory (IRT) might recognize (4) as resembling a two-parameter IRT model (de Ayala, 2022), where λ_j is analogous to what would typically be called a "difficulty parameter," δ_{ij} is similar to a "discrimination parameter," and θ_{it} represents the latent "ability" the model is trying to estimate. However, instead of some cognitive ability, this model estimates a different latent value: the share of each country-year's population that places themselves at each location along the left-right scale or party affect scale.

There are two key differences between this model and a traditional IRT model that help adapt it to this particular use case. First, IRT models typically use a logistic link function to connect the model parameters to the observed data. This is appropriate when the data are binary (for example, a correct or incorrect answer on a test question) but, as I have explained, I need to preserve the full distribution of data and avoid collapsing it into just two response options. I therefore use a softmax function to link the model parameters to the observed, multi-category survey responses. The softmax function is a multidimensional generalization of the logistic function which maps its argument to a probability distribution over response categories. It therefore takes a vector of parameters and outputs a vector of response probabilities, η_{itj}, which sum to one.

Second, I incorporate the three parameters in this latent variable model as random effects, or varying intercepts. Random effects models are typically presented with a compound error term, which encapsulates an additive combination of error from different sources, such as unit-specific variation, time-specific variation, and residual error. Representing the latent variable model in this way leads to a similarly intuitive interpretation. There is some total amount of variation in how survey respondents choose response categories. This total variation can be decomposed into things like the item bias effects, item-country latent effects, and country-year latent effects I described previously. In this formulation, then, λ_j can be understood as item-level residuals, δ_{ij} as item-country-level residuals, and θ_{it} as country-year estimates of the propensity for survey responses to fall into each category, adjusted for item and item-country effects (Claassen, 2019; McGraw & Wong, 1996).

Item bias effects λ_j and item-country latent effects δ_{ij} are modeled hierarchically as a function of data, with response options nested in survey items (for λ_j) and response options nested in survey items and countries (for δ_{ij}), making this a fully hierarchical linear model. In case I only have a small handful of observations for some item types, modeling these effects hierarchically helps prevent those small samples from producing extreme estimates. Just like a hierarchical linear model (Gelman & Hill, 2007), this specification shrinks the estimates toward the mean when sample sizes are small. These parameters take normal priors:

$$\lambda_j \sim N(\mu_\lambda, \sigma_\lambda^2),$$
$$\delta_{ij} \sim N(0, \sigma_\delta^2). \tag{5}$$

Finally, the country-year latent effects θ_{it} must be smoothed over time. One way to do this would be to employ linear interpolation, a method commonly used to estimate missing data points in time series. In linear interpolation, I would use the set of country-years for which I have data and estimate any missing country-years between them by first calculating the slope of the line between existing points and then finding where the missing country-years would fall along that line. Interpolation therefore assumes linearity and is deterministic – it will always give the same solution when data are held constant.

In reality, however, over-time changes in survey responses are neither linear nor deterministic, especially after implementing the latent variable model in (4). I therefore model each country's latent effect estimates as the outcome of a random walk, such that the estimate in each country-year is a function of the previous country-year's estimate, plus random error (Claassen, 2019; Jackman, 2005):

$$\theta_{it} \sim N(\theta_{i,t-1}, \sigma_\theta^2). \tag{6}$$

Instead of taking country-years with observed data as fixed, this dynamic specification models them probabilistically just as it does for country-years without observed data. I can also relax the strong linearity assumption required for interpolation, instead allowing latent effect estimates to follow whatever temporal trend the model deems most appropriate. Because this specification incorporates random error, the trend is not deterministic and will differ slightly with each iteration during model fitting. This variation from one iteration to the next is precisely what enables the model to select the trend that best fits the data.

All three variance terms used previously – σ_λ^2, σ_δ^2, and σ_θ^2 – are held constant across countries, years, and response options; are estimated from the data; and take weakly informative $N^+(0,2)$ priors.[13]

The result of this dynamic latent variable model is a collection of vectors θ_{it} modeled hierarchically, smoothed over time, and adjusted for the key sources of variation I outlined previously. The next challenge is to take these estimates of latent ideology and party affect and recover the distribution of those latent variables. More specifically, I now have model-adjusted estimates of where respondents in each country-year tend to fall on the ideology or party affect scales, given by θ_{it}. However, I need to transform these latent estimates back into a quantity that is easily understood: the number of respondents giving each response option in each country-year.

Doing so is relatively straightforward. Recall that in (4), I used the softmax function to link the output of the latent variable model to the observed survey responses. To recover the predicted response counts from the model-adjusted latent estimates, I simply need to retrace my steps. Pushing θ_{it} back through the softmax function maps those latent estimates to a vector of probabilities, which can then be passed to a multinomial distribution along with the total number of survey responses observed in each country-year to generate $\tilde{y}_{it}$ – a vector of length K giving the number of responses in each country-year-category, corrected for item and country-item effects:

$$\tilde{y}_{it} \sim \text{Multinom}(N_{it}, \text{softmax}(\theta_{it})). \tag{7}$$

These vectors of model-adjusted response counts are directly analogous to the response counts I showed in Section 1, Figure 4 that came simply from the raw data, weighted to be nationally representative.

Figure 5 continues the running example of response counts in the 2016 United States. Just like the plots in Section 1, Figure 5 depicts a histogram of response counts, this time juxtaposing the raw data against the distribution of response counts generated by the latent variable model. The black bars show the raw data – the same distribution as in Section 1, Figure 4 – and the gray bars show the model-adjusted response counts. In general, the distribution of model-adjusted response counts retains the same general properties as the original data; it is a bimodal distribution with one mode centered between zero and twenty on the feeling thermometer scale and another mode centered at approximately seventy. The two modes appear to have approximately the same variance, with the density of response counts in each distribution increasing and decreasing in tandem.

---

[13] Although inverse-gamma or half-Cauchy distributions are sometimes preferred for this type of prior, half-normals provide greater computational tractability and numerical stability.

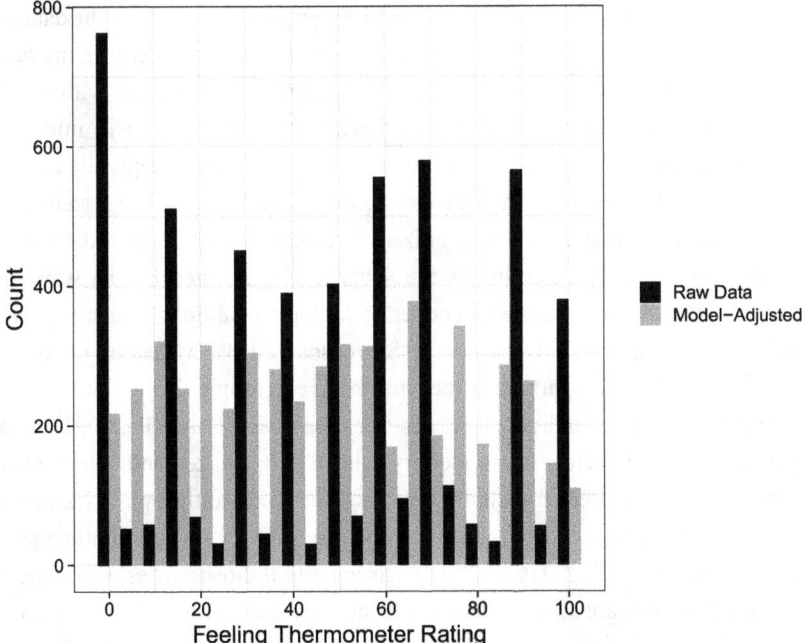

Figure 5 US running example: Comparison of raw data to model-adjusted response counts

There are also a couple key differences that demonstrate the utility of the latent variable model. Perhaps most obvious is that the raw data exhibit a very large number of responses at the extreme low end of the scale; the modal feeling thermometer score in the raw data is zero degrees. As I mentioned previously, certain features of survey implementation and country context might affect where survey respondents place themselves on this scale. After correcting for these sorts of variation, the model-adjusted counts are more spread out across the low end of the scale, instead of being entirely clustered at zero. Also clear from this histogram is that model-adjusted counts are more evenly distributed over response options. This is as opposed to the raw data, where respondents tend to select only feeling thermometer scores in increments of five or ten, even though they have 101 response options available to them. This smoother distribution of responses will be useful in the next step, where I need to fit a continuous model to these ordinal data.

2.4 Uncovering Characteristics of Latent Groups: A Gaussian Mixture Model

The aforementioned model produces adjusted, smoothed distributions of ideology and party affect. But before I can use these distributions to calculate polarization, I need to recover the group structure of each country-year's distribution. That is, I need to know how many groups are present in the data so I can measure polarization as a function of both intergroup heterogeneity and intragroup homogeneity, as I discussed in Section 1. In countries with small party systems such as the United States, this information can be easily inferred. But most countries do not resemble the United States' deeply ingrained two-party system. Instead, they have more fragmented, multiparty systems.

Complicating matters further, citizens' perceptions of parties, their ideologies, and their issue positions are substantially affected by the ways in which parties in these systems cooperate to form coalitions (Adams et al., 2016; Fortunato, 2021; Fortunato & Stevenson, 2013). Measures of affective polarization, in particular, benefit from examining larger clusters of responses instead of individual parties (Kekkonen & Ylä-Anttila, 2021). The frequency with which citizens identify with a party waxes and wanes over time (Dalton & Wattenberg, 2000), citizens often hold multiple party identities (Garry, 2007), and they can feel positively or negatively toward multiple parties at once (Samuels & Zucco, 2018), particularly if those parties' ideological or issue positions are similar distances from one's own (Algara & Zur, 2023).

Measures of ideological polarization are likely affected by similar factors. Citizens frequently take cues from their preferred political elites about where they should stand on issues of the day (Lenz, 2012; Zaller, 1992). The structure of party competition in a given time and place therefore likely affects where citizens place themselves on an ideological scale (Adams et al., 2012a; Zechmeister, 2006). For example, party systems with a strong centrist party or coalition are more likely to beget a critical mass of centrist voters in addition to the more common blocs on the left and right. Alternatively, party systems experiencing a rise in populist right parties, like many places in contemporary Western Europe (Bale & Rovira Kaltwasser, 2021), may even see a newly meaningful cluster of mass-level ideology on the extreme right, in addition to more mainstream right views.

In sum, the complexity of elite-mass linkages can make measuring polarization in multiparty systems a difficult undertaking. Some scholars of affective polarization deal with these challenges by weighting party affect with party vote shares under the assumption that polarization is mostly driven by voters whose primary identification lies with the largest parties (Garzia et al., 2023; Reiljan et al., 2024; Wagner, 2021), setting aside many of the considerations I outlined previously. Other scholars eschew vote share weights and include all parties in the calculation but define affective polarization exclusively as the sum of differences between one's preferred party and all others (Boxell et al., 2024), attempting to graft the United States' unique two-party model on other party systems. Still others consider party systems to be simply a series of party dyads, the sum of which approximates the party system – and all its intricacies – as a whole (Adams et al., 2023; Gidron et al., 2020). In the study of ideological polarization, the most common approach is to ignore the presence of ideological groups entirely and use the variance of a distribution to gauge the degree to which it is dispersed (Lindqvist & Östling, 2010; Lupu, 2016; Rehm & Reilly, 2010). These solutions, while creative, are suboptimal.

To more flexibly extract information about the groups comprising each country-year distribution, I use a Gaussian mixture model to characterize the distribution of model-adjusted response counts $\tilde{y}_{it}$, which I expand into a vector of responses z_{it} of length N_{it}.[14] A Gaussian mixture model assumes that a set of observations – z_{it} in this case – can be represented as a linear combination of two or more normal distributions. It describes a distribution with more than one mode, or "component," in which each component has its own mean and variance parameters, just like any normal distribution. It also estimates the proportion of observations encapsulated by each component, referred to as the "weight" of that component. These weights always sum to one. In this application, I can formally represent the Gaussian mixture model for z_{it} as:[15]

$$p(z_{it}) = \sum_{c=1}^{C} \omega_{itc} \cdot N(\mu_{itc}, \sigma_{itc}^2), \tag{8}$$

where c indexes mixture components. ω_{it}, μ_{it}, and σ_{it}^2 are vectors of component weights, means, and variances, respectively, all of length C. These latter two parameters take the following priors:

$$\mu_{it} \sim N(\bar{z}_{it}, \sigma_{\mu_{it}}^2),$$
$$\sigma_{it}^2 \sim N^+(0, 0.5), \tag{9}$$

where $\bar{z}_{it}$ denotes the mean of z_{it} for each country-year and $\sigma_{\mu_{it}}^2$ further takes a weakly informative $N^+(0, 2)$ prior.

This mixture model therefore allows me to handle many challenges with measuring polarization in multiparty systems. Party systems wax and wane in size, different coalition arrangements develop and collapse, and changes

---

[14] Technical note: Though they effectively contain the same information, mixture models operate more naturally on vectors of individual observations than vectors of response counts. Within each country-year it, I move from the vector $\tilde{y} = \{\tilde{y}_1, \ldots, \tilde{y}_K\}$ to the vector $z = \{z_1, \ldots, z_N\}$ by defining $N = \sum_{k=1}^{K} \tilde{y}_k$ and $z_n = \sum_{k=1}^{K} k \cdot \mathbb{1}_k(n)$, where $\mathbb{1}_k(n) = \begin{cases} 1 & \text{if } n = k \\ 0 & \text{otherwise} \end{cases}$.

[15] Fowler et al. (2023) and Kekkonen and Ylä-Anttila (2021) also use mixture models to recover latent groups in a distribution of political ideology and party affect, respectively, with the former additionally embedding their mixture model in a latent variable model, as I do here.

in these features of the political system show up in citizens' judgments about where they stand on the left-right spectrum or how they feel about each party. The mixture model accounts for this variation by design. It flexibly detects clusters of responses, subsumes smaller parties into components primarily comprised of larger parties, and groups together party families or coalitions whose adherents naturally cluster together. By allowing the model to recognize such features, I can avoid making ad hoc decisions about which parties to include and which to exclude or worrying about how the number of small parties changes over time. Critically, the model also automatically detects the location and dispersion of groups in addition to their size, giving me all the information I need to calculate the degree of polarization in each country-year's distribution of opinion, a task I describe later in the section.

In practice, fitting a Gaussian mixture requires the a priori specification of the number of components C. That is, I would typically need to tell the model how many components are in each opinion distribution, and thus how many means, variances, and weights it should estimate. Specifying this number is straightforward when there is a theoretically clear number of groups but, owing again to the many sources of variation in multiparty systems, the appropriate number of latent components in this case likely varies across countries and years. To allow for this flexibility, I place an upper bound on the total number of components and give the model the freedom to determine the number of components in each country-year up to that maximum.[16]

Any integer would work for the upper bound on C; I merely need to select a reasonable one for this substantive application while keeping in mind that a higher C further increases strain on computational resources. To balance these competing interests, I choose $C = 5$ under the assumption that mass opinion is unlikely to exhibit more than five distinct political groupings. If a political system is characterized by a clear left-right divide, for example, it is likely to have only two main clusters of voters. If there is a strong centrist party or coalition, it may have three clusters. Additional, smaller coalitions or party families may add one or two more clusters but, in most cases, citizens are unlikely

---

[16] Technical note: I implement this model as an infinite Gaussian mixture, implying that the model follows a Dirichlet process. The distribution of z_{it} therefore takes a countably infinite set of component parameters, with most component weights approaching zero in the limit, leaving only those components within which most of the probability mass is contained. ω_{it} is consequently a sparse vector of length C. The degree of sparsity in ω_{it} is controlled by a Beta(1, 4) prior on component weights, where the weights are estimated using a stick-breaking process. Combining this estimation procedure with a prior with so much probability density close to zero helps ensure that the components uncovered by the mixture model do, in fact, represent meaningful clusters of data.

to perceive fine-grained differences in ideology or party affect such that they clearly differentiate themselves in opinion surveys.

Analyzing the number of components uncovered by the model in each country-year reveals three insights. First, imposing $C = 5$ as the maximum number of components appears sufficient. ω_{it4} and ω_{it5} approach zero for most country-years, implying that citizens typically fall into two or three opinion groupings.

Second, the vast majority of country-years are best represented by a two-component distribution; the model identifies only 2.4 percent of ideology distributions as having more than two components. On one hand, this result could be an artifact of the data itself. Left-right self-placement scales typically contain no more than eleven response options, making it less likely that smaller groups of responses can be distinguished from one another. On the other hand, this result could also suggest that citizens tend to simplify political ideology into an easily understood distinction between left and right, at least when it comes to placing themselves on an ideological scale.[17] Distributions of party affect are much more likely to contain distinct groups of responses, with the model identifying 11.7 percent of country-years as having more than two components. Again, this increased prevalence in multi-group distributions could be due to the greater number of response options available to survey respondents (feeling thermometers are typically placed on a scale from zero to 100) or it could reflect citizens' perceptions of individual parties, party families, or coalitions.

Last, examining where and when these multi-group distributions appear provides additional evidence that the model is capturing politically meaningful variation. Relative to majoritarian systems, countries employing proportional representation (PR) are likely to contain a greater number of effective parties (Lijphart, 1994). This pattern shows up in the number of components the model identifies in each country-year. PR systems account for 80.4 and 85.1 percent of country-years with more than two components in their ideology and party affect distributions, respectively. This incidence rate is noticeably higher than the base rate of PR systems, which account for 63.2 and 65.5 percent of all country-years for which I have data on ideological and affective polarization, respectively.

Continuing the running example of party affect in the United States, Figure 6 shows how the mixture model converts a collection of survey responses into a set of component distributions for a given country-year. First,

---

[17] In some cases, they may be much more skilled at identifying where parties lie on the same scale (Fortunato & Stevenson, 2021; Hetherington, 2001).

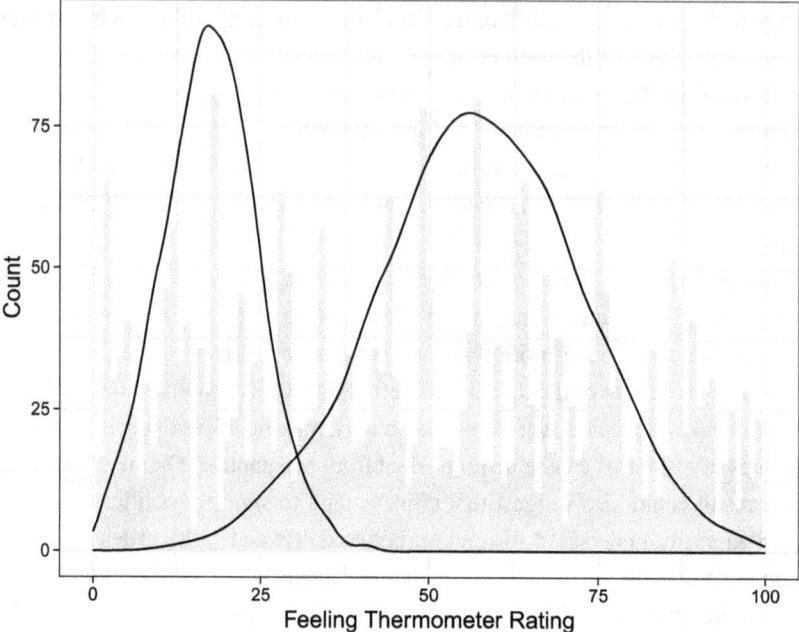

Figure 6 US running example: Modeling feeling thermometer counts with a Gaussian mixture model

I graph the histogram of model-adjusted response counts in the background of the figure. This is the same data as shown by the gray bars in Figure 5, but I graph the histogram with a smaller bin size here to show more fine-grained details of the distribution. Then, I take the output of the mixture model in this country-year and use it to superimpose the density plots of the estimated component distributions. The density plots in Figure 6 therefore represent the final output of the model I laid out in this section. They take raw survey data – weighted to be nationally representative – adjust it for several forms of nonstochastic variation that I do not want to bias the polarization estimates, and use this adjusted distribution of survey responses to recover information about the latent groups present in the data.

In the case of the United States in 2016, the running example throughout this and the previous section has consistently shown clear evidence of two groups present in these data; most respondents who feel warmly toward the Republican Party also feel coldly toward the Democratic Party, and vice versa. Figure 6 shows that even without guidance from the researcher, the model successfully identified this distribution as having two groups. The "cold" group of responses is visible on the left side of the plot, and approximately follows the contours of the histogram. The mean of the histogram and density plots are both around fifteen degrees and these responses are more tightly clustered together.

The "warm" group of responses is visible on the right side and, again, looks similar to the histogram of underlying data used to fit the model. The mean is approximately sixty degrees, and this component is more diffuse, with a greater variance. The density slopes downward to the left along with the histogram until the two normal distributions overlap around the thirty-degree mark.

2.5 Calculating Polarization of Opinion Distributions

The final step in this long process is to compute a measure of polarization for each country-year. To do this, I need to extract parameter estimates from the mixture model: a set of component means μ_{it}, standard deviations σ^2_{it}, and weights ω_{it} in each country-year. These parameters represent the location, dispersion, and size, respectively, of each opinion cluster. My emphasis on estimating both location and dispersion parameters for these opinion clusters is deliberate. The two features of polarization discussed in Section 1 can only be captured by fully parameterizing the latent distribution (Hill & Tausanovitch, 2015; Levendusky & Pope, 2011). I therefore aim to estimate the degree of polarization in the distribution parameterized by μ_{it}, σ^2_{it}, and ω_{it}.

Ideally, a measure of polarization would adhere to the conceptual understanding I presented in Section 1. Scholars often rely on common, easily calculated quantities like difference-in-means or variance to roughly capture the spread of an opinion distribution (Abramowitz & Saunders, 2008; Bischof & Wagner, 2019; Down & Wilson, 2008). Although straightforward to understand and apply, these measures gloss over the conceptual subtleties of polarization. Because they do not capture both intergroup heterogeneity and intragroup homogeneity, they may not be adequate measures of polarization as a group-based concept.

The most popular measurement approach, difference-in-means, approximates intergroup heterogeneity by subtracting the ideological or policy positions of one party from another (Canes-Wrone & Park, 2012; Großer & Palfrey, 2019; Hetherington, 2001). However, this has the effect of data reduction – extremists get rolled into their parties' overall mean, perhaps leading to an estimate of polarization which is biased downward. Moreover, polarization is not merely an increase in distance between the extremes; it also implies some level of concentration around the emerging poles. There can be a wide distance between the two most extreme parties in a given party system but, if voters are evenly dispersed throughout the policy space, that party system will be less polarized than it would be if all party members were in complete agreement. This is one reason why Levendusky and Pope (2011) urge scholars to "go beyond the mean" when measuring polarization.

A second popular measurement approach, more common in comparative politics, is to use standard deviation or variance to approximate the degree to which a distribution of opinion is widely dispersed (Hill & Tausanovitch, 2015; Lupu, 2016; Rehm & Reilly, 2010). Scholars often use variance because it is "the most common measure of dispersion" and "does not depend on whether [data points] are clustered in distinct groups" (Lindqvist & Östling, 2010, p. 546). While true, this operationalization seems at odds with the conceptual understanding of polarization, which emphasizes distinct clusters of opinions as one of the phenomenon's defining characteristics. To reflect the group-based conceptualization I presented previously, a measure of polarization should model those clustering properties directly instead of smoothing over them.

To take full advantage of the rich distributional information I recovered using the measurement model, I apply the cluster-polarization coefficient (CPC). Mehlhaff (2024) explicitly develops the CPC to conform to the group-based conceptualization of polarization. It quantifies both intergroup heterogeneity and intragroup homogeneity and uses them to calculate the degree of polarization in a given distribution. It does so by recognizing that the total amount of variance in a distribution (total sum of squares, *TSS*) can be expressed as the sum of the variance contained *between* the distribution's clusters (between-cluster sum of squares, *BSS*) and the variance contained *within* the distribution's clusters (within-cluster sum of squares, *WSS*):

$$TSS = BSS + WSS. \tag{10}$$

Figure 7 visually depicts how the quantities in (10) map onto the distribution of United States party affect uncovered by the mixture model.[18] *BSS* captures how far apart the distribution's components are, while WSS_1 and WSS_2 capture how concentrated each component is around its ideal point. WSS_1 and WSS_2 are summed to produce the *WSS* term in (10).

The CPC uses these values to produce an estimate of polarization. A simplified version of the adjusted CPC formula,[19] applied to this unidimensional use case, can be expressed as:

$$CPC_{adj} = 1 - \frac{WSS}{TSS} \frac{N_{it} - 1}{N_{it} - C_{it}}, \tag{11}$$

---

[18] This visualization should not be construed as mathematically precise – for example, *BSS* is not literally the distance between component means – but it does offer an illustrative demonstration of how mathematical concepts show up in the distributions I have been working with throughout the section.

[19] The adjusted CPC is used in situations like this one, where the number of dimensions or clusters may vary across units of comparison.

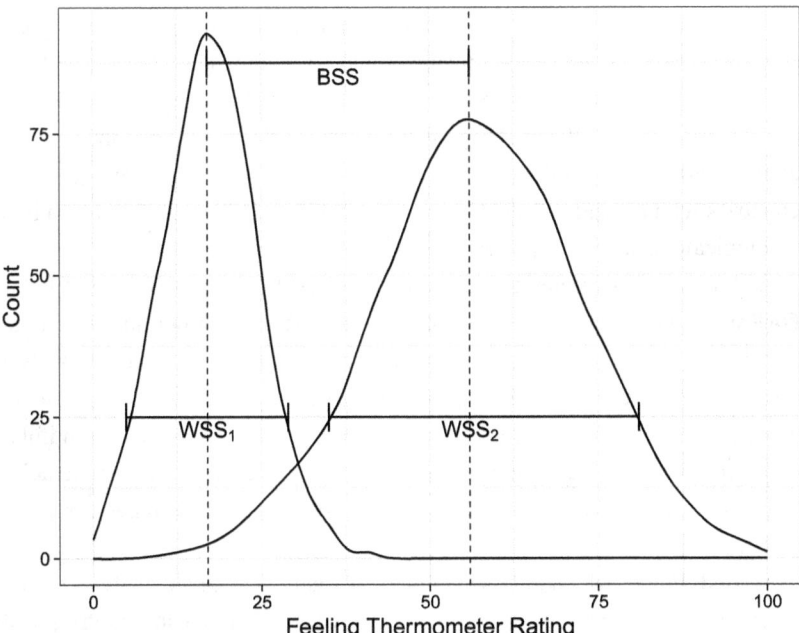

Figure 7 US running example: Distributional features used to calculate polarization

where N_{it} and C_{it} represent the number of observations and clusters, respectively, in each country-year. By correcting for different numbers of groups across country-years, the CPC ensures that polarization estimates are not inflated or deflated as a mere artifact of, for example, over-time changes in the number of parties. By applying the CPC to the distributions of ideology and party affect estimated by the measurement model, I can recover quantitative estimates of polarization that adhere to its conceptual definition. All polarization estimates provided in PolarCAP and used in this Element, therefore, are the result of applying the CPC to the country-year distributions recovered by the measurement model.

2.6 PolarCAP: Smooth Panels of Public Opinion Polarization

The result of the measurement model described in this section is a set of smooth country-year panels of mass ideological and affective polarization. The output of the model is *smooth* because it estimates a distribution of opinion in each country-year over a long period of time with no gaps – even if no survey was fielded in some country-years. The output is a country-year *panel* because, assuming that each country-year's aggregated survey marginals are drawn from nationally representative samples (or are weighted to be nationally representative), the estimated distributions of opinion can be considered panel estimates of each country's aggregate opinion over time (Claassen, 2019).

PolarCAP contains 4,508 country-year estimates of ideological polarization (1971–2019) and 2,340 country-year estimates of affective polarization (1975–2019). Figure 8 depicts the geographic distribution of country coverage among countries with only ideological polarization data available and those with both ideological and affective polarization data.

As I describe in greater detail in subsequent sections, the structure of PolarCAP supports scholarship on polarization in at least three important ways. First, it facilitates apples-to-apples comparison across a wide range of contexts. Even the most comprehensive existing datasets of mass polarization (e.g. Boxell et al., 2024; Gidron et al., 2020) are able to leverage data from only a handful of cases, mostly European countries and other advanced industrial democracies. PolarCAP contains data on as many as ninety-two countries, spread across the globe.

Second, PolarCAP enables scholars to conduct fine-grained analysis of how polarization changes within each country over time. Even in countries with more plentiful and readily available data, existing datasets could only provide quick snapshots of mass polarization in those countries, often with long temporal gaps in between. For example, the Comparative Study of Electoral Systems (CSES) is a popular source of party affect data with which to calculate polarization. But studies relying solely on this data source (e.g. Gidron et al., 2020; Wagner, 2021) have, at most, only four or five time points available to them. PolarCAP contains forty-nine years of data, with polarization estimates available for every year from 1971 to 2019.

Finally, moving beyond descriptive analysis, the smooth panel estimates produced by this model and the close fit between concept and measure enable scholars to test causal theories of mass polarization in a way that so far has not been possible.[20] Not only does the temporal completeness of PolarCAP facilitate the use of sophisticated statistical methods for time series data, but the broad geographic coverage provides enhanced generalizability for the conclusions scholars may draw from those analyses.

2.6.1 Relationship to Existing Measures

In Sections 3 and 4, I dive deeper into PolarCAP estimates. Before I do that, however, it would be helpful to know whether they correlate with some of the

---

[20] On using the output of dynamic latent variable models in causal tests, see Claassen (2020a, 2020b) and Tai et al. (2024).

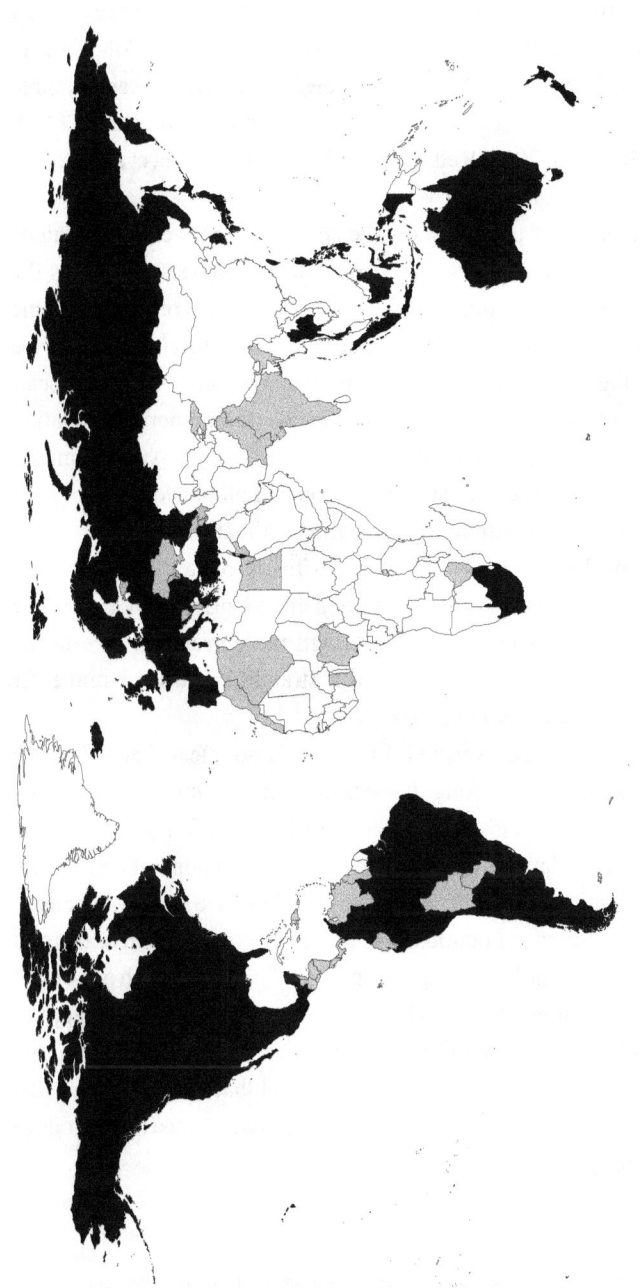

Type of Data ▨ Ideological Only ■ Ideological and Affective

Figure 8 Geographic coverage of final dataset

many existing cross-national datasets of mass polarization. Most studies of ideological polarization in a comparative setting are concerned with polarization among elites or parties – which are not my focus in this monograph – so I evaluate only affective polarization in this analysis. I compare PolarCAP to five existing datasets: Boxell et al.'s (2024) weighted distance measure, three implementations of Reiljan's (Reiljan, 2020) affective polarization index (API; Garzia et al., 2023; Orhan, 2022; Reiljan et al., 2024), and Garzia et al.'s (2023) distance-based measure, taken from Wagner (2021).[21]

Figure 9 uses a matrix of plots to show the correlation between each pair of datasets in a couple different ways. The names of the datasets are across the upper and right axes of the figure, and the individual plots correspond to the bivariate relationship between the corresponding datasets. To visually describe this relationship, the lower triangle of the matrix in Figure 9 displays scatterplots and trend lines. The upper triangle displays the numeric correlation between datasets, in each case using only the subset of country-years common to each dataset pair. Along the diagonal of the matrix, I plot histograms of each dataset to visualize the distribution of polarization estimates.

As made clear by Figure 9, PolarCAP is positively related to all existing datasets. However, the strength of those relationships ranges from a very low 0.098 to a modest but still low 0.259. Although the correlations are in the expected direction, PolarCAP is clearly not a straightforward substitute for existing datasets of affective polarization.

In some ways, this is to be expected. In fact, it is not clear that PolarCAP *should* correlate highly with existing datasets, as there are many features distinguishing it from the alternatives on offer. It estimates a full distribution of opinion as opposed to collapsing opinion into a single ideal point, it corrects for many sources of variation that are known to bias comparative survey responses, it explicitly models clusters of opinion instead of marginalizing over them, it allows citizens' views of parties to shape the nature of polarization in a country-year instead of incorporating many small parties into the analysis, and it applies a more conceptually appropriate measure of polarization to the resulting distribution. These differences are likely impactful; Mehlhaff (2024) shows that when it comes to affective polarization, specifically, existing measures produce conceptually inappropriate estimates.

---

[21] There are several additional datasets of affective polarization developed by other scholars (e.g. Gidron et al., 2020; Wagner, 2021). However, they are not publicly available and it would be nearly impossible to replicate every data processing decision made by the original authors. To avoid misrepresenting these datasets, I analyze only those which have been distributed for public use.

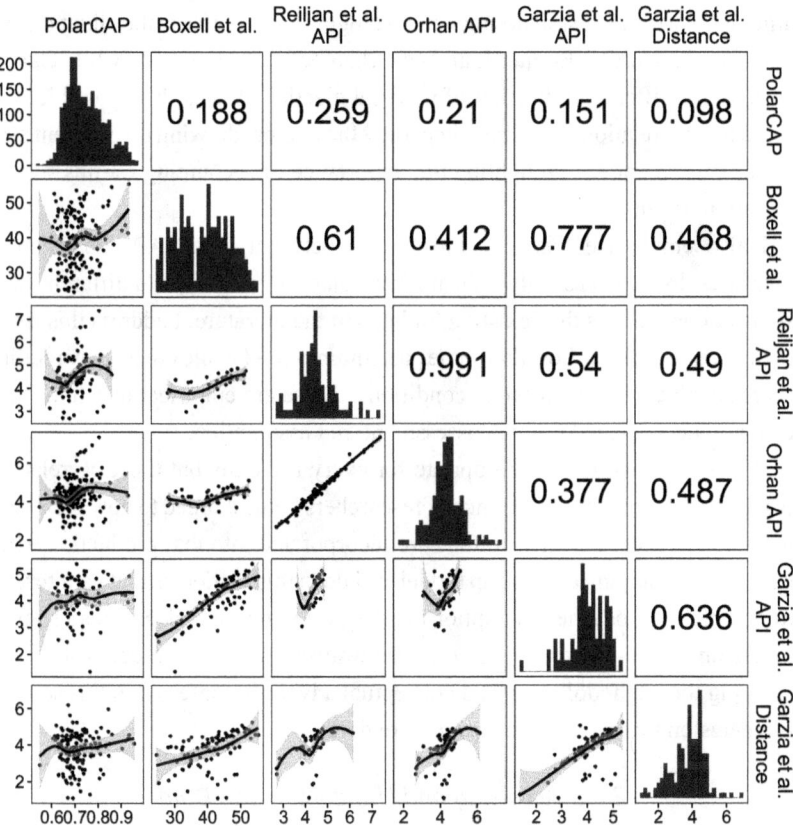

Figure 9 Distributions and correlations of existing affective polarization datasets

Note: Affective polarization datasets listed across upper and right axes. Lower triangle shows trend lines with 95 percent confidence intervals. Upper triangle shows numeric correlations. Diagonal shows histograms of each dataset. All correlations use only the subset of country-years common to each dataset pair.

Moreover, correlations among existing datasets also underperform expectations in many cases. The five datasets I analyze here use similar data sources, employ similar data processing workflows, and apply similar measures of polarization, but eight out of ten pairwise comparisons fail to reach a correlation of 0.7; half do not even eclipse 0.5. Exemplifying this pattern are the three sets of API scores. All three apply the API measure to feeling thermometer data from national election studies. Reiljan et al. and Orhan's estimates correlate very highly, as one would expect. But Reiljan et al. and Garzia et al.'s estimates correlate only at 0.54, and the relationship between Orhan and Garzia et al.'s estimates is even weaker, at 0.377. Such middling correlations – despite the datasets being close replications of each other – highlight the challenges faced by mass polarization scholarship and indicate that the baseline correlation among polarization estimates may not be high. Also notable is the slight difference in data sources; Reiljan et al. and Orhan both use the CSES, while Garzia et al. use a different collection of national election studies. It is possible that these low correlations are driven in part by the authors drawing on different sets of survey programs, highlighting the importance of accounting for this sort of variation as I do.

I also emphasize that low correlations between PolarCAP and existing measures do not necessarily indicate that PolarCAP would yield different substantive conclusions than existing findings in the literature. I address this issue in Section 4, where I show that some past findings hold while others may require more specific theoretical scope conditions. These are empirical questions that can only be answered through assessment, not assumption.

PolarCAP may not be appropriate for every use case, but these correlation results underscore the importance of researchers being attuned to how their data is produced and what assumptions are incorporated into that production. One benefit of employing a Bayesian model, as I do in this section, is that I am forced to be upfront about the assumptions undergirding my model. Scholars should assess on a case-by-case basis whether these assumptions are defensible, but ignoring the methodological and conceptual advances conferred in this section is a decision that would likewise require defense.

2.6.2 Accessing and Using PolarCAP Data

There are two primary ways to access data from the Polarization in Comparative Attitudes Project. The main portal to PolarCAP is the R package of the same name, `PolarCAP`: Access the Polarization in Comparative Attitudes Project, which is available on the Comprehensive R Archive Network (Mehlhaff, 2023). The project's companion website provides short vignettes describing how to incorporate the package into common data analysis pipelines and how to retrieve polarization estimates and associated standard errors for specific country-years (https://imehlhaff.net/PolarCAP). This package recognizes country identifiers in most languages and formats, making it a flexible, user-friendly method for merging PolarCAP estimates into existing data sources. For users not familiar with R or who prefer to work from the full data file, a variety of download formats are available on the same website.

3 Polarization across Time and Space: Descriptive Analyses

Descriptive analysis represents a critical component of social scientific research, providing empirical observations with which to generate or test hypotheses (King et al., 1994; Munger et al., 2021). Accordingly, scholars often seek to understand how country cases compare in their levels of polarization (Handlin, 2017; McCoy & Somer, 2019) or how polarization changes in a country over time (Abramowitz & Saunders, 2008; Adams et al., 2012b). Previous data constraints meant that one could only make such comparisons in a handful of countries or over a few repeated cross-sections within each country. Key benefits imparted by the procedures in Section 2 allow PolarCAP to overcome these constraints and facilitate thorough description. Using a measure that incorporates both theoretical features of polarization and compares across cases with different numbers of relevant groups ensures descriptive inferences are accurate. In addition, building a measurement model that grants broad geographic and temporal coverage allows me to paint the most comprehensive portrait to date of mass polarization around the world.

Examining descriptive patterns also carries implications for the validity of the data collection. Measurement models like the one in Section 2 are necessarily complex. Before forging ahead with all available data, it makes sense to take preliminary steps to illustrate that the data represent sensible trends in polarization.

First, I evaluate how polarization changes in four countries over the course of their time series – Mexico, South Africa, Spain, and the United States – focusing on a small set of significant political or social events. The historical record provides plentiful information about the political context that played out in each of these countries during the period covered by PolarCAP. A sound measure of polarization should reflect such changes in context, so I leverage that information to provide a sense of construct validity. For example, a state that experiences a protracted period of economic crisis and political upheaval might display a higher level of polarization during that period. By contrast, a democratic state ruled by a single party or coalition with widespread electoral support should exhibit a lower level of polarization.

Second, I compare all PolarCAP countries in 1980 and 2010. These snapshots of polarization levels around the world allow me to highlight how mass polarization reflects historical events occurring at these temporal cross-sections. For example, civil war in Central America produced high polarization estimates in 1980, and grand coalitions in the German Bundestag show up in low polarization estimates in 2010. These "apples-to-apples" comparisons at single time points may prove useful in descriptive exercises, as in this section, or as data points in studies using comparative historical analysis.

There are limitations to using historical conditions to validate quantitative measures. Some events might theoretically increase polarization, while other contemporaneous events might decrease it. The events that get noted in the historical record, especially in developing areas, could be systematically biased toward groups who hold power in society (e.g. McCullagh, 2000). My intention is not to use this descriptive exercise as a rigorous validity check, only to show that polarization estimates frequently reflect relevant historical events in ways one would expect. It is also worth noting that, as with any measurement or modeling procedure, there is some degree of error inherent in the final product. For that reason, I focus on general trends in polarization and avoid drawing inferences about small fluctuations that may simply reflect noise in the estimates.

3.1 Temporal Changes in Mass Polarization

A key advantage of PolarCAP is that it enables scholars to conduct fine-grained analysis of how polarization changes within each country over time. Although the full PolarCAP dataset contains information on ninety-two country cases, I select four to examine in greater detail: Mexico, South Africa, Spain, and the United States. In each case, I present a brief historical arc of relevant political events. If measured well, polarization should ebb and flow around the same time these events took place. In selecting these four exemplar cases, I aim to balance geographic range with variation across structural elements such as the economy, party system, electoral institutions, and regime type. Even in this diverse mix of cases, polarization estimates reflect important social and political events in each country's recent history quite well.

3.1.1 Mexico

I begin in Mexico, the most recently democratized country of the four. Although still in the grip of de facto one-party rule when the time series begins in the early to mid-1970s, the 1980s saw a marked increase in organized opposition to the *Partido Revolucionario Institucional* (PRI; Bruhn, 1997). Hastening electoral gains by the *Partido Acción Nacional* (PAN) and *Partido de la Revolución Democrática* (PRD) was a period of economic crisis and poor natural disaster management by the ruling PRI.

As oil prices hit all-time highs in the 1970s, the government attempted to spur continued development by borrowing large amounts of foreign currency against future oil revenues. Mexico's public debt grew by more than thirty percent per year and became unserviceable in the early 1980s, when sharply rising interest rates in creditor countries and a collapse in oil prices led to a debt crisis across the region and a sovereign default in Mexico in 1982 (Golub, 1991). The resulting recession – often referred to as *La década perdida* ("The Lost Decade") – continued through the rest of the 1980s. Public disenchantment with the ruling PRI further compounded when a magnitude 8.0 earthquake struck Mexico City

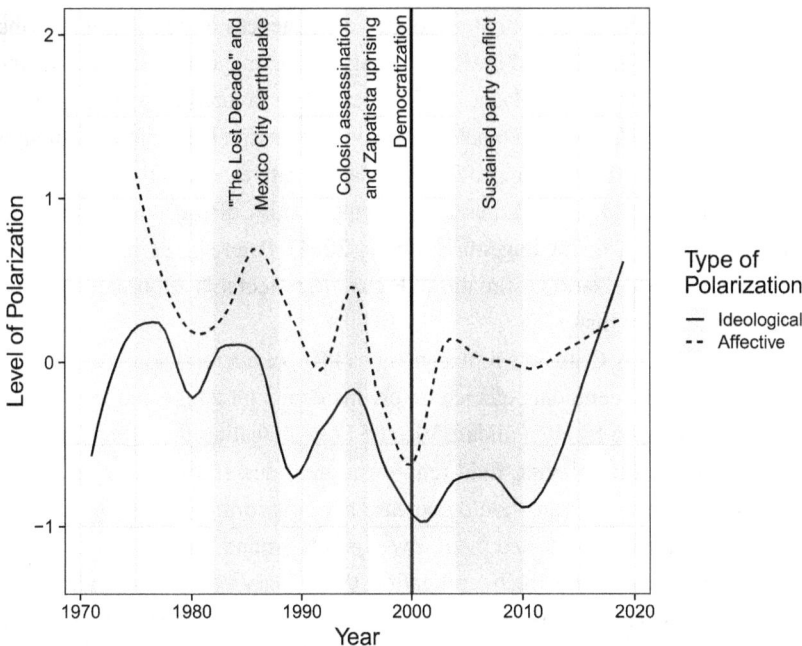

Figure 10 Mass polarization in Mexico
Note: Trend lines with 90 percent confidence intervals. Estimates unit-normalized across countries for purposes of comparison.

in 1985, resulting in thousands of casualties, billions of dollars in damage, and the loss of potable water for most residents. President de la Madrid waited two days before acknowledging the situation, his administration initially declined international aid, and citizens' access to government assistance appeared to be determined in large part by clientelist relationships with the PRI (Anderson, 2011).

Turmoil and dissatisfaction should fuel polarization, as the public's feelings toward the party in power grow more negative and other parties suggest policy alternatives. We see evidence of both in Figure 10, which plots trends in ideological and affective polarization in Mexico. The left-most vertical shaded region corresponds to The Lost Decade and the Mexico City earthquake, and clear local maxima in both ideological and affective polarization are evident in this time frame.

Another brief period of political upheaval ensued in the mid-1990s. On New Year's Day in 1994, the *Ejército Zapatista de Liberación Nacional* (EZLN) – a group of indigenous rebels – declared war on the Mexican state. The EZLN protested indigenous exploitation, land reform, and the implementation of the North American Free Trade Agreement (NAFTA; Stahler-Sholk, 2007).

The uprising drew global attention to the consequences of neoliberal reforms implemented by the PRI and inflicted damage to the image of a stable, modernized Mexico. Two months later, the PRI candidate favored to win that year's presidential election, Luis Donaldo Colosio, was assassinated at a campaign event in Tijuana. Though unproven, popular narratives at the time linked the slaying to high-ranking PRI members unhappy with Colosio's departure from the incumbent president's agenda (Dibble, 2014). Brief spikes in ideological and affective polarization estimates in Figure 10 reflect this tumultuous year in Mexican political history.

Ernesto Zedillo, Colosio's replacement as PRI presidential nominee, proved to be the last PRI candidate elected before the democratizing election of 2000, when voters chose PAN candidate Vicente Fox. Defeating the ruling party on an uneven electoral playing field requires a great degree of consensus in the electorate, so polarization should decrease here. Accordingly, ideological and affective polarization reached their lowest points around 2000.

In the final years before democratization, the primary axis of division in Mexican politics had been attitudes toward the regime. After the PRI's defeat, voters could divide themselves among the parties on offer. The division among parties became apparent during the 2006 election campaign, in which elites exchanged rhetorical barbs in the media and displayed a high degree of inter-party conflict (Bruhn & Greene, 2007). Citizens developed strong attachments to parties and remained loyal to them on election day (Klesner, 2007), with the PAN and PRD presidential candidates separated by less than 0.6 percent of the vote. Elite conflict like that revealed throughout the 2006 election season is likely to reflect heightened affective polarization. PolarCAP estimates in Figure 10 reveal such a trend; affective polarization increased in the years leading up to the election and maintained this level for several years.

3.1.2 South Africa

I turn next to South Africa, another developing, recently democratized country. Apartheid – an extensive system of de jure discrimination and segregation – persisted nearly until the twenty-first century. But by the early 1980s, protest, international pressure, and demographic change made apartheid untenable, and Prime Minister Botha took steps toward dismantling it (Beinart, 2001). Non-Whites received limited legislative representation, Blacks gained labor and urban property rights, expenditures for Black schools increased, and the thirty-year ban on the African National Congress (ANC) was lifted in 1990. This slow march toward reform instigated swift backlash among Whites, resulting in a deeply divided citizenry (Sisk, 1989). Accordingly, a rise in ideological

Mass Polarization across Time and Space

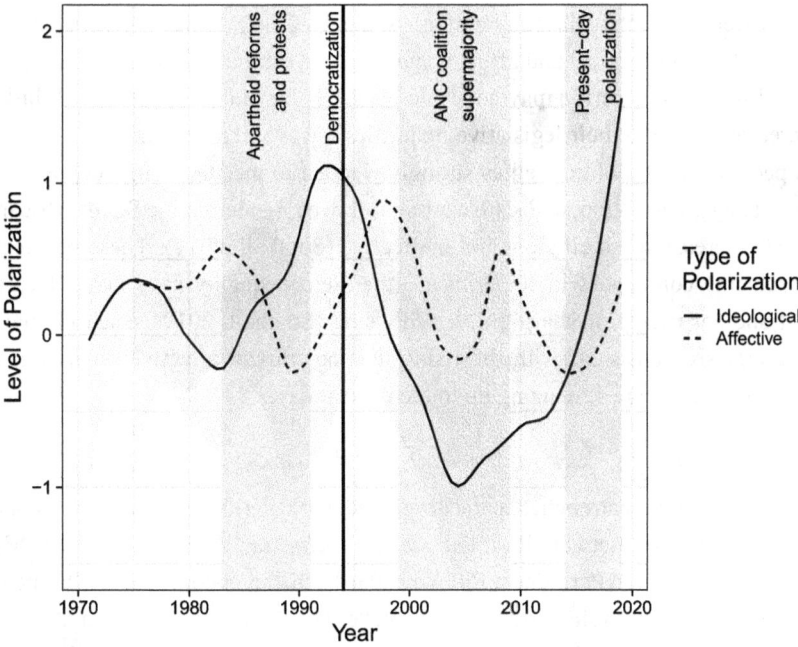

Figure 11 Mass polarization in South Africa

Note: Trend lines with 90 percent confidence intervals. Estimates unit-normalized across countries for purposes of comparison.

polarization can be seen in the left-most shaded region in Figure 11, which corresponds to the period of apartheid reforms and related protests.

Affective polarization estimates did not, however, rise during this period. Since the ANC was outlawed from standing for election and did not officially participate in government, surveys at the time did not ask respondents to give their opinion on that party. This practice, in effect, limited the party affect information gathered by surveys to primarily White voters who chose among the other parties on offer. Affective polarization estimates in Figure 11 increase precipitously after surveys began including the ANC around 1990, reflecting electoral conflict between the National Party and ANC.

The democratizing election of 1994 ushered in legislative dominance by the ANC. Though tensions were still high, as evidenced by the affective polarization estimates in the late 1990s, the political arena was flush with new voters. Either outright or with coalition partners, the ANC held a supermajority in Parliament from 1999–2009. They undertook a reconciliation effort to defuse antipathy in the populace and presided over peace and economic growth (Gibson, 2004). It makes sense that such conditions would occur alongside an extended decline in polarization (Southall, 2019), which is reflected by decreasing ideological and affective polarization estimates in Figure 11.

However, this period may have laid the seeds for future division. With little credible threat to their legislative majorities for two decades, the ANC developed a cadre of political elites strongly wedded to the state. High degrees of patronage, corruption, and state capture followed, rendering the South African state increasingly inefficient and ineffective (Southall, 2014). These political problems, combined with lingering apartheid-era inequality, have sparked fears of another period of sharp political division (Southall, 2019). Such circumstances are consistent with the rising ideological and affective polarization captured in Figure 11 leading up to the present day.

3.1.3 Spain

Though Spain is entrenched in the developed world, its modern political history has not been without volatility. The *Partido Socialista Obrero Español* (PSOE) brought stability to Parliament following the death of dictator Francisco Franco, but cracks began to show by the early 1990s. The PSOE, historically a Marxist party, lost its affiliation with the labor movement and allied with the Catalonian nationalist bloc *Convergència i Unió* (CiU), demoralizing supporters and sparking fears that the CiU would push for Catalonian independence (Encarnanción, 2008). Several corruption scandals, including financial fraud and extrajudicial killings to combat Basque terrorism, further undermined support for the PSOE (Jiménez, 2004). PolarCAP data capture the period of corruption and growth of the Spanish right in Figure 12, showing heightened ideological and affective polarization between 1988 and 1996.

The conservative *Partido Popular* (PP) succeeded the PSOE as ruling party in 1996 and achieved an absolute majority in 2000, in an election revealing little substantive difference between the two major parties (R. S. Chari, 2000). Polarization estimates dip at this time point in Figure 12, as might be expected in a period of economic growth and party similarity.

However, political missteps mobilized the left and ensured the PP's fortune was short-lived. The government's decision to send troops to Iraq was opposed by a large majority of the public. The protests it sparked in 2003 were the largest anti-war demonstrations in Europe and, at the time, likely the largest protests in Spanish history (Heywood, 2003). In response, the PP blamed opposition parties and claimed to be victims of political terrorism (Blakeley, 2006).

Crisis mismanagement compounded the issue. The PP government made little effort to mitigate the *Prestige* oil spill, and they misled the public about the scope of the disaster (R. Chari, 2004). Madrid train bombings killed nearly 200 people days before the 2004 election, and both the PP and PSOE responded by

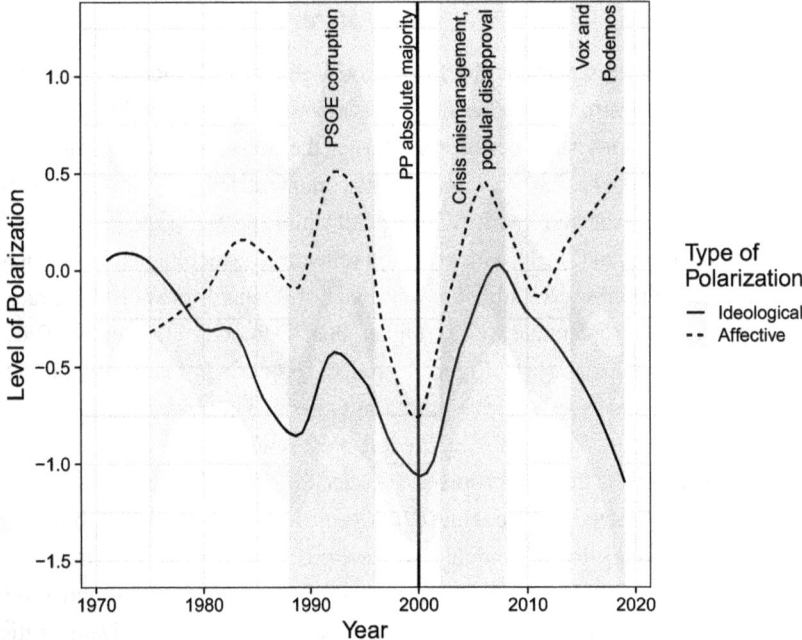

Figure 12 Mass polarization in Spain

Note: Trend lines with 90 percent confidence intervals. Estimates unit-normalized across countries for purposes of comparison.

accusing the other of distorting information for electoral gain (Blakeley, 2006). The PP insisted Basque separatists were behind the attack, even long after evidence made clear that al-Qaeda was responsible. This episode prompted more protests, and voters handed the reins back to the PSOE in the next election. Figure 12 suggests that both ideological and affective polarization rapidly increased in this period of elite conflict and disenchantment with the ruling party.

Though polarization abated slightly during the PSOE's rule, the protracted financial crisis (2008–2014) and the more recent rise of extremist parties *Vox* and *Podemos* are again stoking fears of affective polarization (Torcal & Comellas, 2022). Though Spaniards are grievously divided when it comes to their political identity, disagreement on programmatic matters remains much lower (Miller, 2020).[22] This combination of high affective polarization and low ideological polarization is captured in the right-most shaded area in Figure 12, which commences just after the founding of *Vox* and *Podemos*.

---

[22] Mass ideological polarization in Spain increased during the COVID-19 pandemic (Ares et al., 2021), but that time period lies outside the scope of this data collection.

3.1.4 United States

The United States is perhaps the most prominent, well-studied case of contemporary polarization, but other periods of rising mass polarization preceded the current one. One such period was during the presidency of Ronald Reagan, whose 1980 election was a watershed moment for the American conservative movement and sparked historically high polarization in Congress Poole and Rosenthal (2001). Mass opinion reflected the ideological fervor permeating 1980s politics. Republicans approved of Reagan's presidency at rates more than sixty percentage points higher than Democrats (Kernell & Rice, 2011). PolarCAP estimates in Figure 13 reflect this period of partisan conflict. They capture a steady rise in ideological and affective polarization throughout Reagan's presidency, delineated by the left-most shaded region.

The latter half of the 1990s sowed the seeds of further polarization. Newt Gingrich was elected to the House of Representatives in 1978, bringing with him a strategy to draw ideological contrasts between parties, nationalize politics by tying Democratic candidates to President Clinton, and force legislative gridlock for which, he reasoned, voters would blame the Democratic

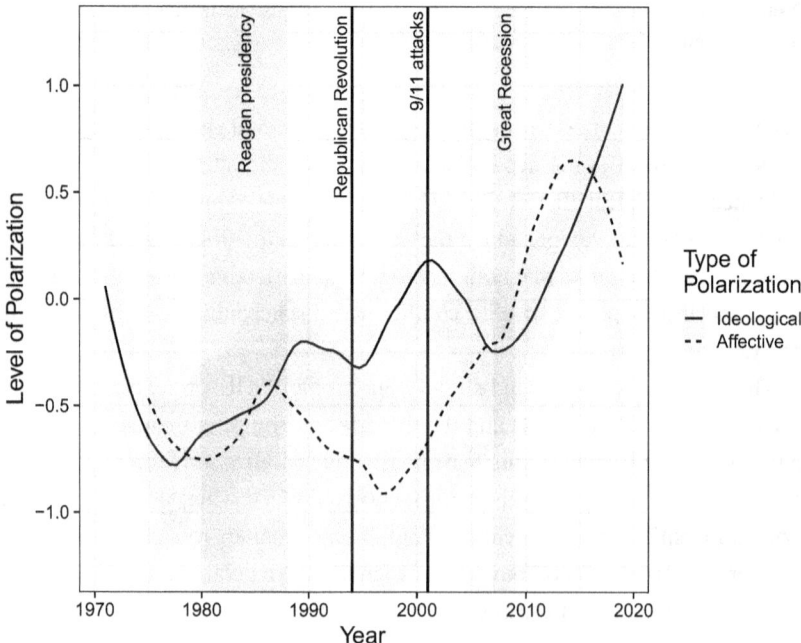

Figure 13 Mass polarization in the United States
Note: Trend lines with 90 percent confidence intervals. Estimates unit-normalized across countries for purposes of comparison.

Party (Rosenfeld, 2018). It proved effective. The "Republican Revolution" saw Republicans take control of the House for the first time in forty years (Aldrich & Rohde, 2000), with Gingrich as speaker from 1995 to 1999. The Republican Revolution also represented the start of a trend toward perennially thin majorities in Congress and high-stakes elections. Such intense competition incentivizes less interparty cooperation, more focus on public relations and messaging, and conflictual public dialogue (Lee, 2016). Gingrich himself disregarded social norms in his public and congressional speeches, describing Democrats as greedy, traitorous, and dishonest (Mason, 2018).

It stands to reason that this era would spur ideological and affective polarization in the mass public. Partisans tend to take cues from their preferred political elites (Lenz, 2012), so differentiation among parties seems likely to lead to ideological polarization among citizens. Accordingly, Figure 13 indicates that ideological polarization began increasing shortly after the Republican Revolution and continued climbing until the early 2000s. In addition, as might be expected in a period defined by party competition and hostile political rhetoric, Gingrich's speakership coincided with the beginning of the precipitous rise in mass affective polarization that would continue for more than two decades.

Ideological conflict abated slightly in the early 2000s, a decade defined by the war on terror. The attacks on September 11, 2001, triggered the highest presidential approval ratings in American history (Lambert et al., 2011), and a staggering majority of Americans – 88 percent in October 2001 (Bowman, 2008) – supported the war in Afghanistan. The war in Iraq likewise garnered high support at the outset, with 72 percent support in March 2003 (Newport, 2003). This broad agreement on the most salient issue of the day manifests in Figure 13 as a decline in ideological polarization.

This decline was short-lived. The 2007–2008 financial crisis thrust the country into the worst economic recession since the Great Depression, and the incumbent Republican Party was punished at the polls in 2008, with Barack Obama claiming the presidency. Though he lacked the harsh rhetoric of Newt Gingrich or Donald Trump, who would succeed him in the White House, Obama's presidency proved to be a time of deepening polarization. Some of his signature policy achievements, like the Affordable Care Act, were implemented unevenly depending on which party controlled each state legislature (Conlan & Posner, 2016). Dysfunction in Congress made efficient lawmaking difficult after Republicans regained the House in 2010. As a result, Obama leaned more heavily on unilateral presidential policymaking (Lowande & Milkis, 2014), drawing the ire of Republican lawmakers, media personalities, and voters (Reeves & Rogowski, 2022). Unsurprisingly, Figure 13 shows a steep rise in ideological and affective polarization following the recession.[23]

3.2 Geographic Variation in Mass Polarization

In the previous subsection, I showed how PolarCAP can be used to track ideological and affective polarization within countries over a long span of time. The fine-grained country-year estimates provided by PolarCAP enable the use of large-N statistical methods and allow scholars to causally identify important relationships. Equally important, however, is that PolarCAP facilitates broad geographic comparison and small-N comparative historical research. To demonstrate, I zoom out and examine how countries' levels of polarization compare at two discrete time points, one near the beginning of the time series (1980) and one closer to the end (2010). The temporal distance between those cross-sections shows mass polarization in two very different historical contexts. In 1980, the third wave of democratization was well underway, the United States and the United Kingdom were transitioning to conservative governments, and the Soviet economy was grinding to a halt. Three decades later, the Middle East was on the brink of the Arab Spring, the developed world was digging itself out from the aftermath of financial crisis, and China had supplanted Russia as the major world power in the East.

Figure 14 depicts the level of ideological polarization in 1980 for each of the ninety-two countries in the dataset. To simplify the illustration, polarization levels are grouped into quintiles and shaded accordingly, with darker shades indicating more severe polarization and lighter shades indicating less polarization. In the same manner, Figure 15 displays levels of affective polarization in 1980 for each of the fifty-two countries for which data availability permits estimates of affective polarization.

Notably, this cross-section provides a snapshot of mass polarization in the middle of the Central American crisis of the 1970s and 1980s and, as a result, this region exhibits an especially high concentration of polarized countries (Weeks, 1986). In fact, El Salvador and Nicaragua were among the most ideologically polarized countries in the world in 1980, according to PolarCAP estimates. A cursory glance at contemporaneous political events suggests why: The Salvadoran Civil War began with a coup in 1979, and the early 1980s saw

---

[23] As in the Spanish case, ending the data collection in 2019 has consequences for polarization estimates toward the end of the time series. The dip in affective polarization from 2015 to 2019 replicates previous studies (e.g. Gidron et al., 2020). However, the data collection does not incorporate information from the contentious 2020 election, which would likely pull affective polarization estimates upward.

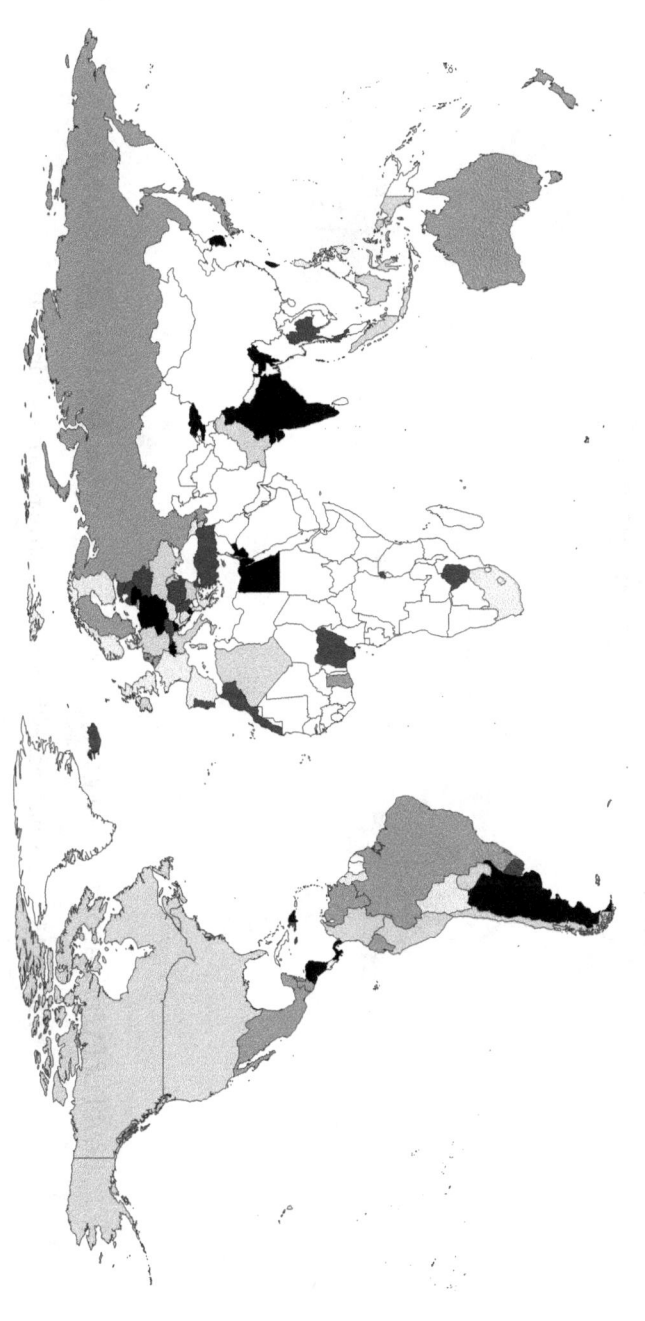

Level of Polarization Very Low | Low | Moderate | High | Very High

Figure 14 Cross-national estimates of ideological polarization in 1980

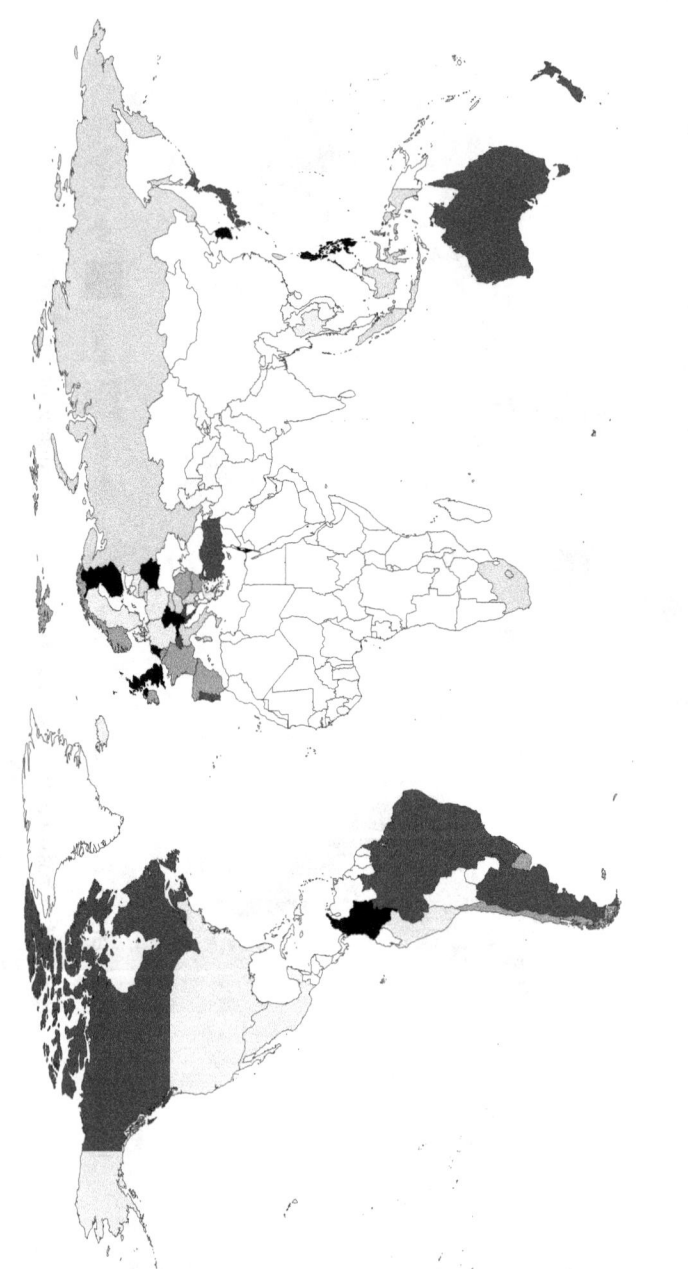

Figure 15 Cross-national estimates of affective polarization in 1980

the recruitment of students, workers, and other members of civil society into the *Frente Farabundo Martí para la Liberación Nacional* (FMLN), the coalition of left-wing groups engaged in guerrilla warfare against the military government. Martín-Baró (1989, 8) describes the early 1980s in El Salvador as being characterized by "social polarization, that is, the displacement of groups toward opposite extremes, with a resultant rigidification of their respective ideological positions and pressure exerted upon everyone to align himself or herself with 'us' or 'them'" (see also Chávez, 2017).

Nicaragua experienced similar tumult. The *Frente Sandinista de Liberación Nacional* (FSLN), a rebel organization, ousted President Somoza in mid-1979, ending the family dynasty that had ruled Nicaragua since 1937. By this point, the country was already more than a decade into the revolution. Another decade of war and instability followed, entrenching Nicaragua in an extended period of extremism and polarization (Barnes, 1998; McCoy & McConnell, 1997).

Thousands of miles away in Scandinavia, Sweden was exhibiting much less severe polarization. For much of the twentieth century, Sweden was a model of governmental and economic stability (Strom, 1986). The Social Democratic Party received over forty percent of the vote – in a proportional system with many parties – in every election from 1932 to 1988. It governed continuously from 1932 to 2006, save for brief interregna from 1976 to 1982 and 1991 to 1994 (Therborn, 2018). Compared to the rest of Europe, Sweden's party system in the 1980s had very low incidence of extreme or anti-establishment parties (Abedi, 2002). Sweden boasted near-full employment, a globally competitive open economy, generous welfare programs, and very low rates of income and gender inequality (Huber & Stephens, 2001; Therborn, 2018). A lack of extreme parties, a fractured political right, and stable social democratic government should produce mild levels of polarization. Appropriately, PolarCAP estimates identify Sweden as one of the least affectively polarized countries in 1980, and only a middle-of-the-pack case of ideological polarization.

PolarCAP's global map of polarization in 2010 looks much different. By this point, the locus of severe polarization had largely shifted away from Central America and toward – among other places – the Middle East and North Africa, which were teetering on the brink of the Arab Spring. Figure 16 displays levels of ideological polarization and Figure 17 shows levels of affective polarization in 2010.

High polarization was not confined to the Middle East, however. Polar-CAP estimates indicate Thailand was among the most polarized countries in 2010. After a coup in 2006 and one year of military rule, civilian government returned to power in 2007. Democracy provides a forum for political conflict that military regimes often repress, allowing political contention to be

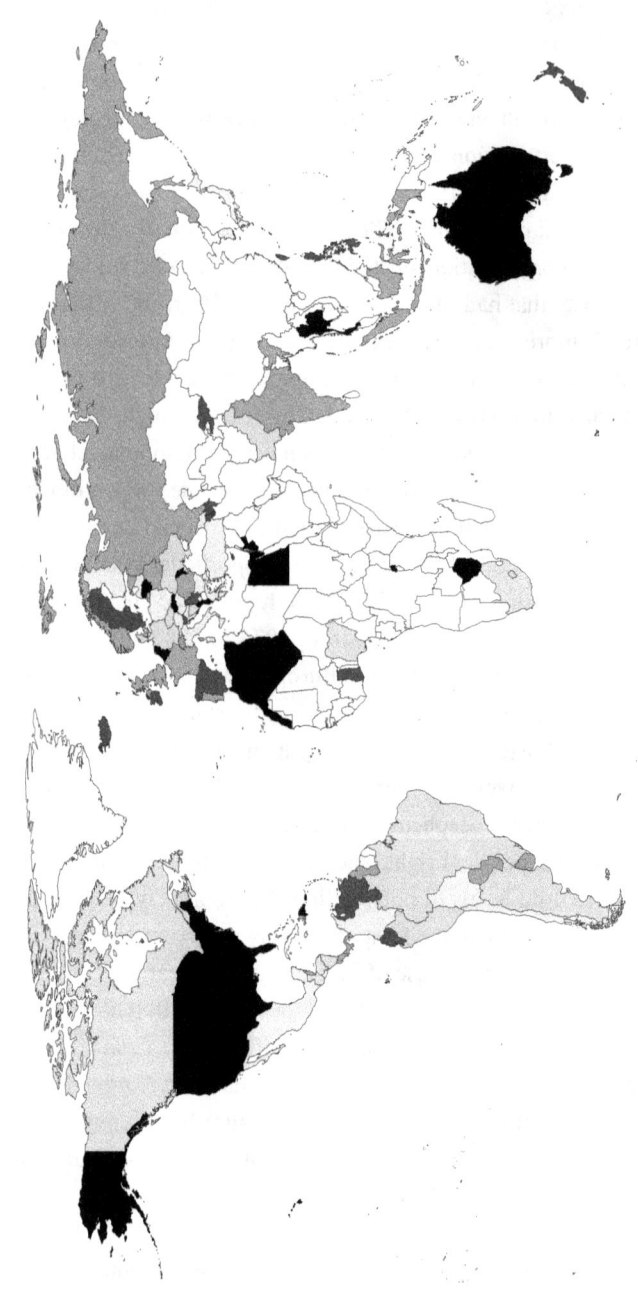

Figure 16 Cross-national estimates of ideological polarization in 2010

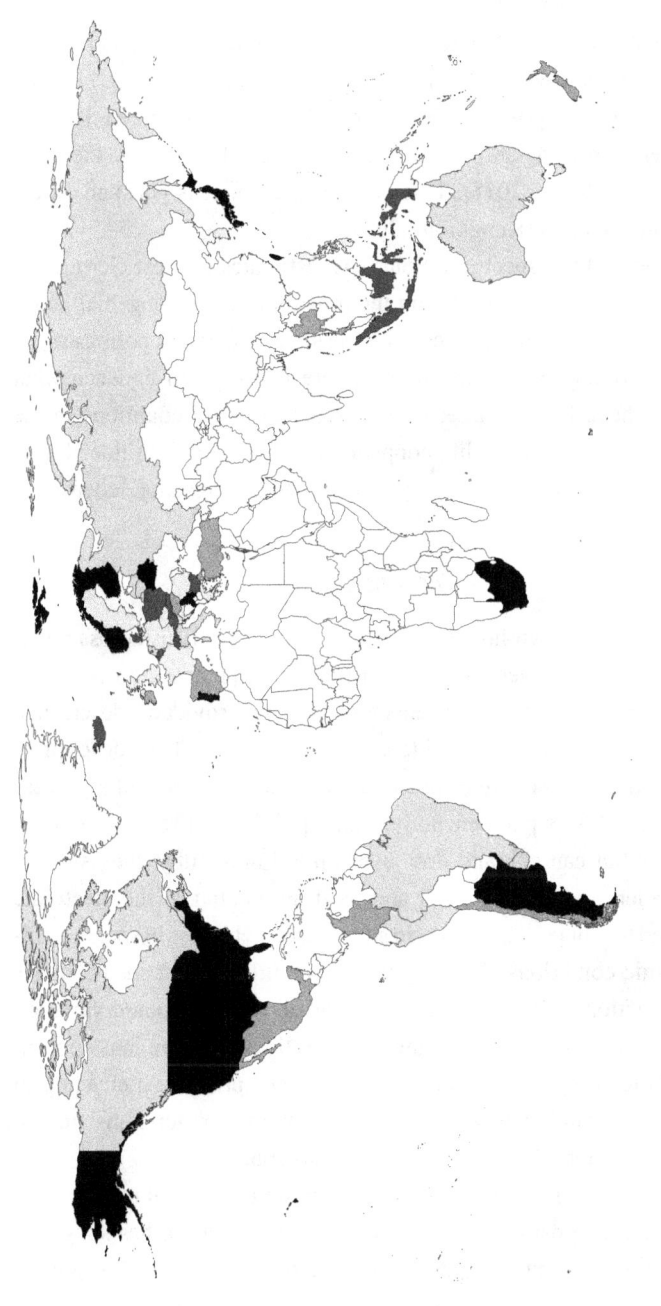

Figure 17 Cross-national estimates of affective polarization in 2010

much more visible. In Thailand, this contention took the form of two political advocacy organizations clashing well into the 2010s: the United Front for Democracy Against Dictatorship (UDD) – which opposed the 2006 coup – and the People's Alliance for Democracy (PAD), a pro-monarchy group which sought to depose the leaders of the civilian government (Dalpino, 2011). The 2010 protests, organized primarily by the UDD, saw an estimated 120,000 protesters descend on Bangkok, leading to violent crackdowns by the military (Human Rights Watch, 2011). This elite-mass conflict is part and parcel of polarization in Thailand (Kongkirati, 2024).

On the other end of the spectrum, PolarCAP estimates suggest Germany – Europe's largest economy – was among the most politically congenial countries in 2010. This estimate aligns well with the state of German politics at the time. In 2010, Germany was experiencing a rare interregnum between what would otherwise have been a sixteen-year stretch of grand coalitions in the Bundestag (Voigt, 2019). Such elite cooperation is reflected in milder levels of mass polarization, which have largely extended to the present (Hebenstreit, 2022).

3.3 Discussion

In this section, I have shown how PolarCAP facilitates analysis across countries and within countries over time, demonstrated that polarization estimates frequently reflect historical events in sensible ways, and provided a descriptive analysis of mass polarization in a wide array of contexts. These descriptive results portray a detailed picture of polarization as both a state and a process (DiMaggio et al., 1996), a phenomenon of mass politics that reflects contemporaneous events but can ebb and flow over time. Importantly, they suggest patterns for further study: Ideological and partisan conflict in the electorate appear to respond to – or perhaps spark, in some cases – changes in social, political, and economic conditions. Precisely which conditions elicit such changes is the topic of Section 4. But at a more basic level, this systematic variation should provide some confidence that these data reliably capture mass polarization, and that the group-based definition in Section 1 provides a meaningful framework for understanding how distributions of public opinion translate into the more intuitive notion of polarization in the mass public.

These data also reveal insights that may be surprising in light of recent work. For instance, much comparative research on mass polarization has sought to place the American case in comparative perspective and to answer, among other questions, whether the United States is truly an egregious case of polarization. Gidron et al. (2020) and Reiljan (2020) find that the US is, in fact, a middle-of-the-pack case of affective polarization, less polarized than other politically stable countries in Europe and Oceania. Boxell et al. (2024) also show that the United States registers polarization scores comparable to at least a couple other industrially developed, consolidated democracies, though they also note it evinces the fastest rate of increase in their small sample. The results presented in this section at least partially contradict these previous conclusions, suggesting that the United States has, indeed, experienced a very high level of mass polarization over the last decade. Whether this intense polarization is a function of the unique set of political institutions in the United States or whether it may pose a danger to democracy in the country are questions for future (and ongoing) research, and I only begin to broach them in the next section.

4 Correlates of Mass Polarization

It is important to gain a clearer picture of how mass polarization varies across cases and waxes and wanes over time. Even more important might be answering questions like: What factors may lead to polarization? How can polarization affect important aspects of social and political life? What types of reforms might hold promise for mitigating polarization when it arises? Are such reforms necessary in the first place, or is polarization a relatively benign feature of democratic politics?

Particularly since the turn of the century, scholars' dedication to answering these types of questions has increased dramatically. Researchers have pointed toward elite behavior (Hetherington, 2001), gerrymandering (McCarty et al., 2009), descriptive representation (Adams et al., 2023), and a host of other potential correlates of mass polarization. Outside the academy, a cottage industry of non-profit organizations has emerged, purporting to decrease polarization by providing spaces for Americans to communicate across political divides.[24]

The spatiotemporal breadth and yearly estimates of mass polarization provided by PolarCAP allow scholars and practitioners to comprehensively assess the correlates – or causes and effects, given an appropriate identification strategy – of mass polarization in a way that has previously not been possible. In this section, I take a step toward assessing these relationships, focusing on three key structural domains: political economy, institutional design, and democracy. The enhanced generalizability and statistical power afforded by the time series estimated in Section 2 and described in Section 3 enable more reliable tests of prominent hypotheses related to each set of correlates. The methodological

---

[24] See, for example, organizations such as Braver Angels, Living Room Conversations, and Build Up.

approach I employ here is rudimentary, relying primarily on pooled correlations and difference-in-means estimates, but it illustrates how these data open doors for future work to investigate empirical relationships more rigorously. With respect to some variables, such as democracy, results provide renewed confidence in old theories. With respect to others, such as income inequality, they suggest the need to impose scope conditions on – or reevaluate entirely – prominent theories of polarization.

4.1 Political Economy

Economic conditions are frequently offered as explanations of ideological disagreements or partisan hostility. Indeed, the positioning of economics as a key determinant of individual-level opinion and macro-level political trends has a long history in the social sciences (Lipset, 1960; Meltzer & Richard, 1981), and the economy's role in shaping distributions of preferences plays a key part in more recent explanations of policy and regime dynamics (e.g. Acemoglu & Robinson, 2006; Huber & Stephens, 2012). Here, I focus on two macroeconomic conditions that may be expected to shape political polarization in the mass public: inequality and unemployment.

4.1.1 Income Inequality

As inequality and polarization in the United States coevolved over the last few decades, scholars amassed an influential literature positing a link between the two. Much of this work investigates the relationship at the elite level, linking both national- and state-level inequality with rising polarization in the United States Congress (Barber & McCarty, 2015; Bonica et al., 2015). McCarty et al. (2006) argue that high income inequality produces sharp divergences between the policy preferences of low- and high-income voters, with the former voting for the Democratic Party and the latter for the Republican Party throughout much of the post–New Deal era. This mass polarization is reflected in elite behavior, as elected officials aim to adhere to the economic interests of their constituents. Gelman (2009) and Rehm (2011) buttress this theory with individual-level evidence of party identification and voting behavior.

Several scholars contend that this relationship generalizes beyond the United States. McCoy and Somer (2019) point out that inequality likely increases the degree to which polarizing elite rhetoric resonates with the masses, as those who feel left behind seek to elect governing officials who will be responsive to their concerns and those who are advantaged by inequality seek to preserve their privileged status. Empirical evidence, however, is mixed.

Gidron et al. (2020) and Grechyna (2016) find support for this theory in studies of cross-national affective and ideological polarization, respectively, but Iversen and Soskice (2015) argue that the relationship between inequality and mass polarization is actually negative. Gunderson (2022) supplies scope conditions that may help explain this discrepancy; he shows that parties' issue positions are only responsive to inequality if parties are well-sorted on the basis of income and economic issues are highly salient during the election.

I examine this possible relationship by taking advantage of country-year data on disposable (post-tax, post-transfer) income inequality, measured with the Gini coefficient (Solt, 2020a). I lag inequality by one year, under the assumption that economic changes affect only future levels of polarization. I further break down the results by regime type (Coppedge et al., 2020), as citizens may react to economic downturns differently depending on the extent to which their interests can be reflected in the political system. Closed autocracies, especially, may exhibit different dynamics, as the lack of multiparty elections means that all political conflict is defined in relation to the regime instead of diffused among multiple parties. Figure 18 displays the correlation between each type of mass polarization and income inequality globally and within each regime type.

Overall, ideological polarization does appear to track with income inequality ($r = 0.117$). However, breaking the results down by regime type reveals important variation. Contrary to the hypothesis developed in the context of the US Congress, ideological polarization in the mass public has a weak – but statistically significant – negative association with inequality in liberal democracies ($r = -0.053$). This mimics the pattern found by Iversen and Soskice (2015) in a sample of consolidated democracies in Western Europe and suggests that one of the mechanisms pinpointed by McCarty et al. (2006) to explain legislative polarization may not generalize to other liberal democracies. Curiously, however, hybrid regimes and closed autocracies evince the opposite relationship, with ideological polarization positively associated with inequality in all three regime types, with two such correlations statistically significant.

Affective polarization results display less of a clear pattern. Overall and in both liberal and electoral democracies, affective polarization does not correlate with inequality. Electoral autocracies are the only context in which the theorized connection appears ($r = 0.125$). The divergence from previous results highlights the value of having complete, smooth time series of polarization. Relying on only a handful of observations for each country, scattered over a period of many years, may return results that break down upon closer inspection.

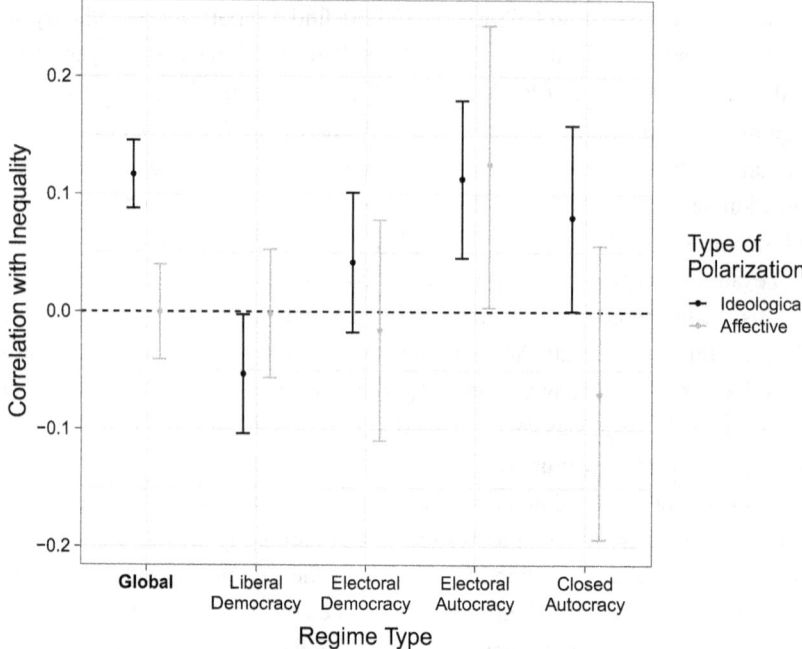

Figure 18 Correlation between income inequality and mass polarization by regime type

Note: Inequality is lagged by one year within each country. Error bars give 95 percent confidence intervals.

4.1.2 Unemployment

Inequality tends to be a stickier, slower-moving economic indicator, with effects that may take several years to accrue. Economic crisis, on the other hand, is a more sudden phenomenon that may inflame political tensions in the short-run. Stewart et al. (2020) argue that when economic conditions are bad, citizens cope with their resultant risk aversion by pursuing safer, in-group relationships and avoiding riskier, out-group interactions, resulting in sociopolitical polarization. Other work has shown that economic downturns spur the rise of radical right parties and result in a more ideologically and affectively polarized electorate (e.g. Funke et al., 2016; Hobolt & Tilley, 2016).

Here, I focus on unemployment, an especially salient economic indicator for average citizens. Because unemployment directly shapes their interaction with the economic and political arenas, it might be expected to track closely with political polarization (Gidron et al., 2020; López & Ramírez, 2004). To test this expectation, I link the polarization estimates with data giving the total percent of the labor force that is unemployed in each country-year (*World Development Indicators*, 2021). As with inequality, I lag unemployment by one year.

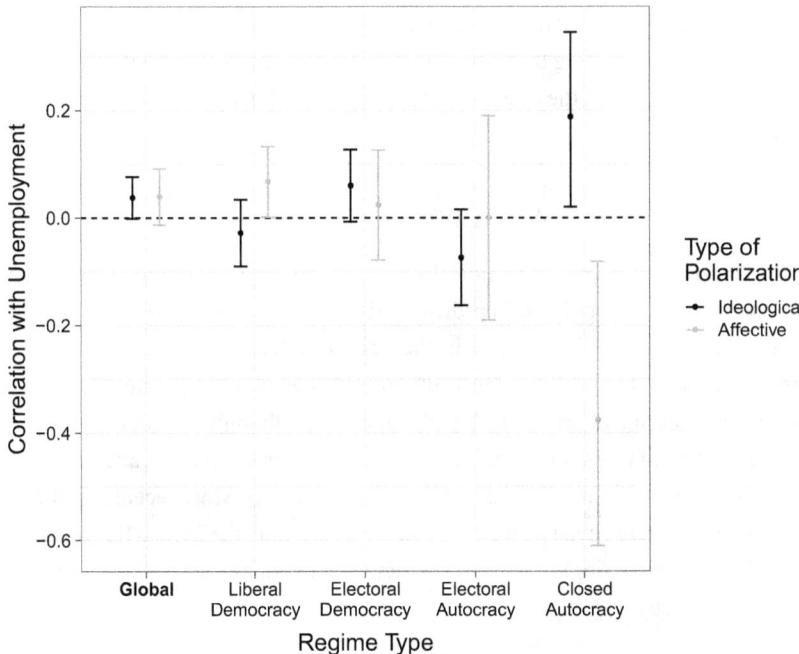

Figure 19 Correlation between unemployment and mass polarization by regime type

Note: Unemployment is lagged by one year within each country. Error bars give 95 percent confidence intervals.

Figure 19, which plots the correlation between polarization and unemployment across regime types, provides weak support for the theory linking polarization to unemployment. Both ideological and affective polarization are positively correlated with unemployment globally, but those correlations are quite small – just under 0.04 for both ideological and affective polarization. However, these weak associations at the global level belie significant variation across regime types. Liberal democracies, which are often more economically stable, show negative but equally small correlations between unemployment and ideological polarization. Meanwhile, the inverse relationship exists in closed autocracies, where higher unemployment exhibits a statistically significant association with more severe levels of ideological polarization ($r = 0.188$).

Results for affective polarization further demonstrate the need to carefully specify scope conditions in theories of mass polarization. In liberal democracies, affective polarization is positively associated with unemployment, just as Gidron et al. (2020) and others argue. But this result generalizes poorly outside democratic states, which contribute the overwhelming majority of cases to existing datasets of affective polarization. In hybrid regimes, affective polarization exhibits no meaningful relationship with unemployment. In closed autocracies, the association is strong, negative, and statistically significant ($r = -0.376$), suggesting that although citizens may disagree about how to deal with economic crisis, they nevertheless grow united in opposition to the ruling party.

4.2 Institutional Design

Time-variant economic indicators like inequality and unemployment appear to operate on mass polarization differently in different contexts, but perhaps a more consistent influence lies in the very structure of politics and governance. The idea that particular institutional designs may shape the distribution of preferences and degree of political contention – though not often articulated in the context of mass polarization – has been prominent in the academic literature for quite some time (Lijphart, 1984; Sartori, 1976). More recently, political commentators have even pushed for electoral reform in the United States, blaming the country's single-member districts for encouraging polarization (e.g. Drutman, 2020).

4.2.1 Executive Type

One such institution with the potential to shape mass ideology and party relations is that of the executive. Linz (1990) famously argued that presidentialism introduced a variety of pathologies into political systems where it was implemented.[25] He reasoned that the zero-sum nature of presidential elections, the frequent lack of a mechanism to resolve conflict between the executive and the legislature, and the rigidity of a president's fixed term length lead to higher-stakes elections, stoke political tension, and incentivize the use of polarizing rhetoric to achieve policy goals. Bünte and Thompson (2023) and Stepan and Skach (1993) echo Linz's concern that the institutional particularities of presidentialism often produce executives who use polarizing rhetoric to attack political parties and the legislature. Political elites' use of divisive language is likely to filter down to their supporters and manifest in heightened affective polarization (Iyengar et al., 2012; McCoy et al., 2018).

Further, the winner-take-all method used to select presidents tends to disincentivize coalition-building, splintering the party system and electorate (Mainwaring, 1993). Though her focus is on the US Congress, Lee (2016) argues that polarization is one possible byproduct of high-stakes elections like

---

[25] This literature is principally concerned with democratic consolidation and survival, but contributing scholars place significant emphasis on polarization as a byproduct of these institutions which, in turn, may contribute to democratic instability.

these. Similarly, Somer (2019) argues the 2017 constitutional change implementing an executive presidential system in Turkey was not only the *result* of an intensely divided electorate but also *led* to further polarization after it was implemented.

However, other scholars have presented arguments suggesting presidentialism may not have such detrimental effects on political relations. Though indeed more rigid than parliamentarism, presidential systems may nevertheless foster conciliation and consensus-building, which would theoretically correspond to lower levels of polarization. Horowitz (1990) contends that because the presidency is a national, popularly elected office, presidentialism provides an incentive for parties in multiparty systems to cooperate to elect a mutually agreeable candidate, promoting moderation and preventing excluded parties from trending toward extremism (on coalition-building in presidential systems, see also Cheibub et al., 2004; Curini & Hino, 2012).[26] When parties take more moderate positions and refrain from attacking each other during election season, the mass public is likely to follow suit. The result ought to be lower levels of ideological and affective polarization.

Horowitz also points out that most evidence suggesting the polarizing tendencies of presidencies comes from Linz's examination of Latin America and Europe, with the former largely employing presidential systems and the latter parliamentary ones. Moving beyond these two regions, however, may yield different results. Parliamentary systems appear to be less correlated with a conciliatory political culture in post-colonial Asia and Africa (Horowitz, 1990; Shugart & Carey, 1992), and ideological polarization and executive type appear unrelated in Eastern Europe and the former Soviet states (Ishiyama & Velten, 1998). Both geographic and temporal variation are likely important for getting an accurate picture of the relationship between polarization and executive institutions (Bell, 2018; Power & Gasiorowski, 1997).

PolarCAP is well suited to satisfy this need for spatiotemporal variation. Figure 20 depicts how polarization estimates vary across executive type classifications (Cruz et al., 2021). I exclude closed autocracies from this analysis, as any variation in executive institutions in these regimes is often mere window dressing for personalist authoritarian rule.

With respect to ideological polarization, the "perils of presidentialism" hypothesis appears to stand on firm ground, even expanding beyond Europe and Latin America. Parliamentary systems are substantially less ideologically polarized than presidential ones. The level of ideological polarization in

---

[26] Faundez (1997) offers Chile as one historical case where this dynamic appears.

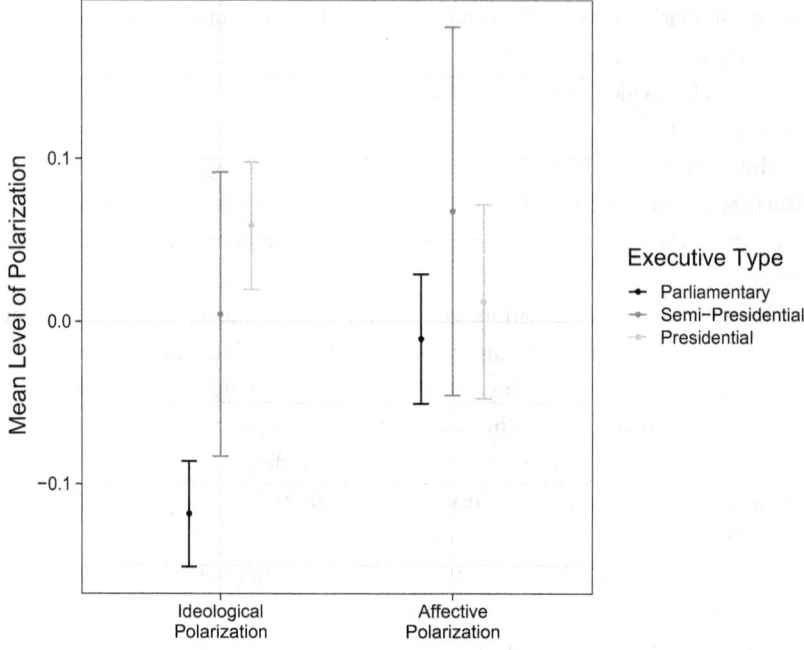

Figure 20 Mass polarization by executive type

Note: Polarization estimates unit-normalized. Error bars give 95 percent confidence intervals.

semi-presidential systems falls right in between parliamentary and presidential estimates but, with a relatively small number of semi-presidential cases in the sample, it is difficult to conclude whether this estimate is truly different from the other two system estimates. Affective polarization, on the other hand, shows no statistically significant difference across executive types. Semi-presidential systems appear much more polarized than parliamentary or presidential systems, but the small number of cases in this category again precludes any firm conclusions. Although presidential systems do promote greater ideological polarization in the mass public, it is not clear that this effect extends to citizens' feelings about the parties.

4.2.2 Electoral Institutions

Electoral institutions might also shape polarization, independent of the executive. Seminal works in political science and economics established that the design of electoral institutions affects the number of parties that a system can sustain and where those parties position themselves ideologically. Duverger (1954) showed that plurality voting with single-member districts favors a two-party system, and Downs (1957) argued that two-party systems will tend toward ideological moderation while multiparty systems are more likely to be ideologically fragmented or polarized, an argument later echoed by Sartori (1976).

More than a half-century on from Duverger and Downs, however, exactly how these electoral particularities and their consequent party system characteristics manifest in mass polarization is still disputed. In line with Downs and Sartori, much empirical work suggests that more proportional electoral systems – for instance, proportional as opposed to majoritarian representation or greater district magnitude relative to single-member districts – result in greater party system polarization and more political extremism (Cox, 1990; Dow, 2011). The intuition is as follows: In a unidimensional spatial model, parties often seek to secure more votes by moving toward the ideological center. But they also want to avoid drifting too far, as the gain in vote share might be relatively small and the resulting policy could be too different from their ideal point. In disproportionate systems, a small change in vote share can lead to a large change in seat share. Hence, greater disproportionality increases parties' incentives to propose a moderate platform, as they have much more to gain from a small increase in vote share. Inversely, in more proportional systems, parties might have more to lose from moderating and are thus incentivized to distinguish themselves. Such ideological differentiation is likely to be reflected in the mass public, manifesting in greater ideological (if not affective) polarization.

Other scholars, however, come to different conclusions. Curini and Hino (2012) show electoral systems that produce more proportional results tend to have *less* severe polarization, so long as the likelihood of post-election coalition formation remains high. Ishiyama and Velten (1998) likewise show a negative correlation between district magnitude and polarization in Central and Eastern Europe. Ezrow (2008, 2011) persuasively argues there is no evidence to suggest that the proportionality of electoral institutions has any effect on party extremism, though his analysis does suggest that citizens in more proportional systems may *perceive* less polarization among parties, which may then be reflected in lower levels of polarization in the mass public.

To contribute to this debate, I merge the polarization estimates with yearly data on each country's electoral system. I use two indicators: the type of electoral system (proportional, majoritarian, or mixed) and average district magnitude (Teorell et al., 2019). I focus on the lower house in countries with bicameral legislatures, and I exclude closed autocracies as I did in the analysis of executive type.

Figure 21 displays the mean levels of ideological and affective polarization in electoral systems with proportional representation, majoritarian representation, and a mix between the two. There is virtually no difference in ideological

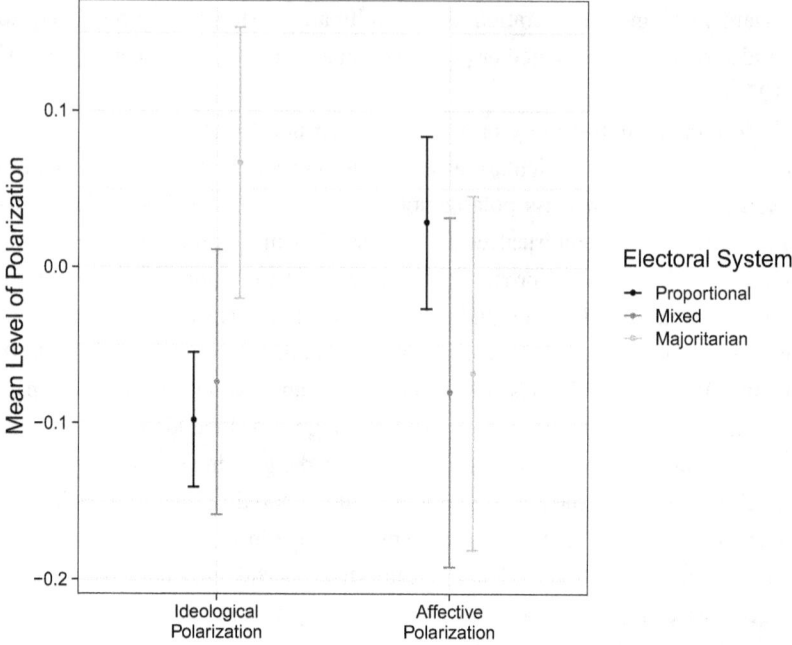

Figure 21 Mass polarization by type of electoral institution

Note: Polarization estimates unit-normalized. Error bars give 95 percent confidence intervals.

polarization between mixed systems and proportional ones, but majoritarian representation is associated with more severe ideological polarization compared to proportional representation, providing additional support for the argument first made by Downs and Sartori decades ago. This heightened ideological polarization does not, however, seem to translate into greater affective polarization; all three electoral system types are well within each other's 95 percent confidence intervals, suggesting the degree to which citizens' interests are reflected in the legislature is largely decoupled from their feelings about the parties competing for their vote.

Figure 22 probes the question from a slightly different angle, displaying the correlation between mass polarization and average district magnitude in the lower house, and further breaking down the results by type of electoral system. The key takeaway, however, is the same: Ideological polarization is positively associated with more proportional electoral results. Globally, greater district magnitude is positively correlated with ideological polarization, and this relationship appears in both proportional and majoritarian systems. Affective polarization displays no such relationship; its correlation with district magnitude across the entire sample is almost zero, and although there is a small

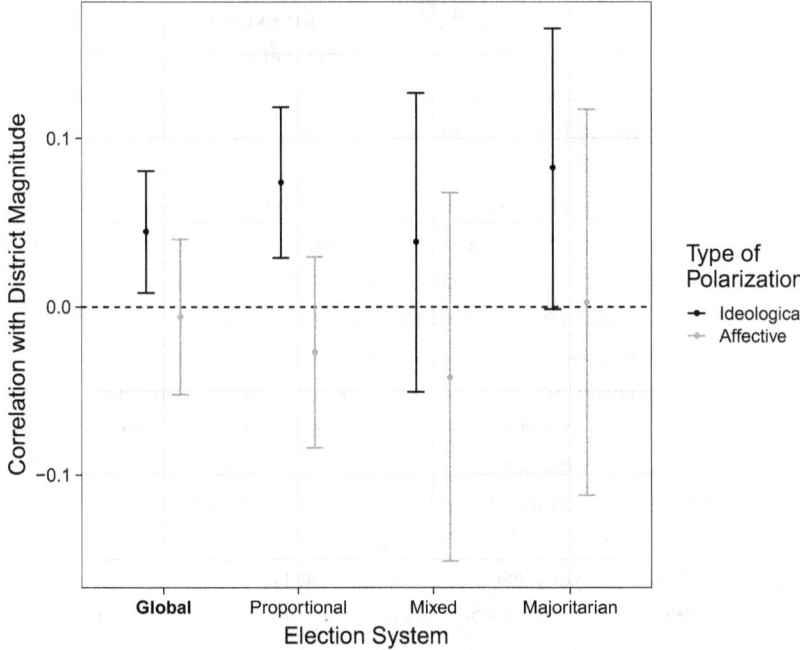

Figure 22 Correlation between district magnitude and mass polarization by type of electoral institution

Note: Error bars give 95 percent confidence intervals.

negative correlation in proportional systems, it is still statistically indistinguishable from zero. The extent to which political institutions diffuse power and representation among a larger share of the electorate seems to have, at most, a minor effect on citizens' tendency to group together in mutually disliked political tribes.

4.3 Democracy

The final set of correlates I examine relates to the degree or quality of democracy in a country. Landmark studies of democratization and political institutionalization point to a contentious political climate as partially responsible for democratic breakdowns and troubled democratic transitions throughout the mid- to late-twentieth century (Huntington, 1968; O'Donnell & Schmitter, 1986). This interest in the intersection of polarization and democracy has enjoyed renewed attention as populist rulers have swept into power across the developed world (Bale & Rovira Kaltwasser, 2021).

In political societies dominated by antagonistic interparty relations, "the polarization, the centrifugal drives, and the tendency toward irresponsibility and outbidding" place democratic regimes at risk (Linz, 1978, p. 24). Citizens in these polities might be more likely to vote for extreme or confrontational candidates (Abramowitz & Webster, 2016; Finkel et al., 2020), decrease their support for democratic norms (Kingzette et al., 2021; Simonovits et al., 2022), or express less dedication to accountability (Graham & Svolik, 2020; Svolik, 2020).

Some empirical research, however, casts doubt on these hypotheses. Across five experiments, Broockman et al. (2023) find no evidence for the apparent connection between affective polarization and democratic attitudes. Voelkel et al. (2023) present two additional experiments with the same null findings and conclude that past work has substantially overestimated the strength of the purported relationship. Finally, Weyland (2020, fn. 13) provides a possible explanation for why mass polarization might not translate into democratic backsliding. He notes that when societies are evenly divided, each party is limited in the amount of popular support they can win. With more voters dedicated to one party or another and fewer ideologically moderate voters who are willing to switch party loyalty each election cycle, it is difficult for any one party to win the legislative seats or votes necessary to make any significant changes to democratic institutions.

I adjudicate between these conflicting viewpoints by combining polarization estimates with democracy indicators provided by the Varieties of Democracy Project (V-Dem; Coppedge et al., 2020). I focus on the two main V-Dem indices – electoral and liberal democracy – as well as a small handful of more specific indicators that are both relevant to the level and quality of democracy in each country-year and could plausibly be affected by polarization. These indicators include the degree to which the political opposition is subjected to repression, intimidation, or harassment; whether election monitors indicated the presence of vote fraud; the degree to which civil society organizations (CSOs) are repressed; and the degree to which the high court makes independent judicial decisions, free from political pressure.

Figure 23 shows how ideological and affective polarization correlate with each of these democracy indicators. Ideological polarization typically exhibits stronger correlations than affective polarization, but substantive results are consistent across all indicators: More severe polarization is associated with lower levels of democracy. This relationship appears in the high-level indices of electoral and liberal democracy – both types of mass polarization display negative, statistically significant correlations with these democracy indices. It also appears with respect to more specific democratic infractions. Polarization is associated with more allegations of vote fraud by election monitors and lower levels of judicial independence from political pressure. It displays normatively undesirable relationships with critical components of liberal democracy

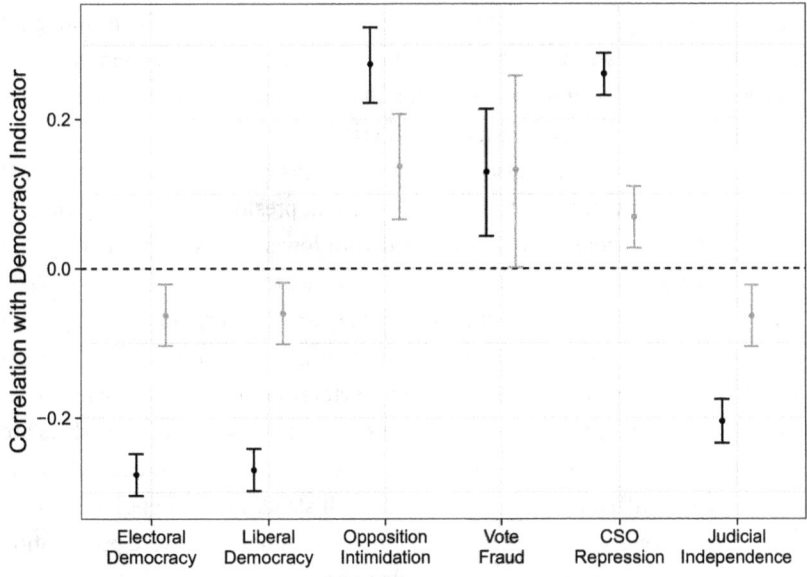

Figure 23 Correlation between democracy indicators and mass polarization
Note: Error bars give 95 percent confidence intervals.

as well; polarization is associated with greater intimidation and harassment of opposition groups and more drastic repression of CSOs such as interest groups, labor unions, and social movements. These strong, consistent results provide additional fodder for the ongoing public debate on the threat posed to liberal democracy by mass polarization, and they bolster the argument made by many comparative political scientists: Mass polarization and democracy struggle to coexist.

4.4 Discussion

The analyses in this section are methodologically simple, but they provide valuable evidence of the structural underpinnings of mass polarization. Perhaps most important, PolarCAP data enable me to generalize results or open a window into variation across space, time, and institutional structures more reliably than has previously been possible.

Results suggest that ideological polarization is related to key indicators of economic well-being, but not always in the ways predicted by existing theory. Income inequality is positively correlated with polarization globally, but that result is largely driven by strong positive correlations in electoral and closed autocracies; in liberal democracies, the relationship is actually negative (see also Iversen and Soskice, 2015). Unemployment has no such effects, though it is associated with stronger ideological polarization in closed autocracies. It is precisely this type of subgroup variation that is not only rarely visible in existing datasets of mass polarization, but is critical for developing sound theory. Ideological polarization is also related to elements of institutional design and democratic quality. It tends to be more severe in presidential and majoritarian systems, and it is consistently associated with lower levels of democracy and more infractions against elements of liberal democracy.

Affective polarization, on the other hand, tracks much less closely with economic and institutional variables. Stronger affective polarization is associated with higher income inequality in electoral autocracies and with lower unemployment in closed autocracies, but correlations with these variables are negligible at the global level, and there is no significant difference in polarization across different types of institutions. Instead, affective polarization is much more strongly associated with democracy, with more severe polarization portending lower levels and quality of democracy.

Some of the results reported in this section, including those concerning inequality, at least partially contradict past theories and evidence. Such a mismatch might be attributable to prior analyses being limited in geographic or historical scope. In this case, the results presented here may not invalidate past theories as much as they suggest the need to impose theoretical scope conditions and more closely specify how the theory might work differently depending on institutional context.

These possibilities are especially likely in the case of income inequality and ideological polarization. Why do different results arise in different geographic regions? Do regime types or institutional variation provide moderating effects? Are historical legacies at play in the minds of citizens (Pop-Eleches & Tucker, 2017)? Perhaps polarization is not a response to declines in absolute levels of economic indicators, but rather is a response to perceived relative deprivation with respect to neighboring countries (e.g. Power et al., 2020).

Inferential caution is similarly in order with respect to affective polarization. Its lack of strong covariation with economic and institutional variables may not necessarily suggest that it is wholly disconnected from these structural elements, but rather that it may be causally downstream from ideological polarization. That is, majoritarian electoral systems may have a centrifugal effect on ideology in the mass public, and the resulting ideological polarization then develops into affective polarization some time later. Indeed, a cursory glance at the polarization time series provides some evidence for this – affective polarization in each country-year is positively correlated with ideological polarization in the previous country-year. Though this correlation is not substantively large

($r = 0.053$), it is statistically significant ($p = 0.01$) and the effects may compound over time. Even the analyses of affective polarization returning ostensibly null findings would therefore be consequential; they would suggest efforts to cultivate a more conciliatory political culture by reforming institutions or restructuring the economy may not be as effective as their proponents hoped (e.g. Drutman, 2020), and a better course of action might be to address ideological extremism directly.

5 Advancing the Scientific Study of Polarization

Scholars of comparative politics have long considered political polarization a key variable in a variety of topics. Linz (1978) described it as a threat to the liberal democratic order. Rustow (1970) saw it as a critical phase through which polities must pass on the way to a successful democratic transition. Sartori (1976) employed the term "polarization" in yet another context, describing one possible configuration of party systems. More recently, with the rise of populism across multiple continents (Mudde & Rovira Kaltwasser, 2017), acute polarization in high-profile cases like the United States (Mason, 2018), and renewed concern for the stability of liberal democracy (Lührmann & Lindberg, 2019), interest in polarization is once again on the rise.

This heightened interest has coincided with the causal inference revolution in the social sciences (e.g. Imai, 2011), yet efforts to causally link mass polarization to other important concepts have proceeded slowly. Manipulating polarization outside the context of a self-contained survey experiment is ethically suspect, and observational data is often too sparse to take full advantage of natural experiments or longitudinal designs. Though causal identification is beyond the scope of this volume, PolarCAP data can and should be leveraged to help gain traction on those questions.

At the same time, an important objective in developing PolarCAP is to bring a more uniform foundation to a rather fragmented literature. Scholars use a wide variety of datasets, many of which provide meager country-year coverage or do not closely reflect polarization as a concept. Scholars of affective polarization, in particular, tend to use similar raw data sources (most frequently the Comparative Study of Electoral Systems) but re-calculate polarization estimates for each individual project, leaving behind a menagerie of datasets that are all slightly different from each other and may give different answers to substantive questions (see, among others, Boxell et al., 2024; Garzia et al., 2023; Gidron et al., 2020; Orhan, 2022; Reiljan, 2020; Wagner, 2021). As I highlighted in Section 2, even when authors use the same data and measure, their resulting datasets may not correlate highly with each other. Working from a common standard facilitates the accumulation of scientific knowledge. I aim to provide such a common standard by sketching a theoretical argument for understanding polarization as a group-based phenomenon and developing a dataset with broad coverage and strong fealty to this group-based conceptualization.

In this concluding section, I take stock of the literature on mass polarization as both dependent and explanatory variable, identify past findings that scholars might consider revisiting with these newly available data, and highlight some substantive questions that can now be asked and answered more rigorously. What follows is a non-exhaustive overview of the literature,[27] though one that I hope sparks new, innovative ideas for other scholars.

5.1 Political Institutions

Perhaps the most urgent question in the minds of scholars, journalists, and politically attuned citizens is whether mass polarization puts countries at risk of democratic backsliding. Much of the foundational scholarship on democratic transitions and breakdowns identified polarization as a threat to democratic consolidation (Huntington, 1968; O'Donnell & Schmitter, 1986), but recent macro-level evidence has largely come from case studies and syntheses thereof (Lieberman et al., 2019; McCoy et al., 2018; McCoy & Somer, 2019). Some analysts even attempt to throw cold water on this otherwise hot research area. Bermeo (2003) shows that voters did not migrate to extremist parties during the twentieth-century democratic breakdowns experienced across Europe and South America. Lowande and Rogowski (2021) argue that polarization actually places an upper bound on the extent to which major crises can result in executive aggrandizement, and Weyland (2020, fn. 13) explains that such an upper bound may follow mechanically from the distribution of party support in a polarized polity. When a party system is egregiously divided, it is difficult for any one party to attract enough votes to win the legislative seats necessary to make significant changes to democratic procedures.

Causal evidence linking polarization to democratic backsliding remains thin. However, with large-scale data collections such as PolarCAP and the Varieties of Democracy project (Coppedge et al., 2020), it may now be possible to identify a causal effect of mass polarization on democracy, and vice versa. Scholars should also dig deeper into causal mechanisms and variables which may moderate the likelihood of polarization leading to backsliding. For instance, legislative gridlock often occurs alongside polarization and democratic breakdown; does it play a role in one or the other? Does it magnify the effects

---

[27] I refer the reader back to Section 4 for discussion of additional variables that may be related to mass polarization.

of polarization on democracy, or is its co-occurrence merely a coincidence, unrelated to either variable?

Instead of looking at only the *level* of democracy – a somewhat coarse indicator – scholars might also examine aspects of democracy's *quality*, such as representation or accountability. Bornschier (2019) suggests polarization played a positive role in new South American democracies. By clarifying the menu of electoral alternatives on offer, Bornschier argues polarization strengthened party-voter linkages and forced parties to remain responsive to voter preferences. Ahler and Broockman (2018) provide evidence for the counter-intuitive view that elite-level polarization enables elected officials to better represent their constituents, even if the citizens they represent are less polarized than they are. But to what extent are these findings unique to the institutional settings – twentieth-century South America and twenty-first-century United States, respectively – in which they are examined? Does the benefit of polarization for accountability degrade in democracies with more institutionalized party systems than those in South America? Does its benefit for representation travel outside the United States' first-past-the-post, single-member district electoral system?

Similarly, if institutionalized party systems are a critical linkage between citizens and their elected officials, it would be helpful to understand how polarization relates to party system institutionalization (PSI). Existing research in this vein is scarce, but two case studies begin to explore potential links. Enyedi (2016) shows that the combination of polarization and high PSI posed a threat to democratic consolidation in Hungary,[28] and Rahman (2019) uses the case of Bangladesh to argue that low PSI can open the door to polarization around conflicting conceptions of national identity. In a large-N analysis, Mainwaring and Bizzarro (2018) hypothesize that party system polarization should be positively related to PSI but find no empirical relationship between the two. But high PSI in Latin America is still relatively low by global standards; adding data from Europe, North America, and beyond may provide a more representative glimpse of global party systems and a wider range of PSI over which to test the theory. A time series analysis with the broad spatio-temporal scope provided by PolarCAP may give different results and provide scholars a valuable window into how mass polarization is reflected in party system polarization, how they collectively contribute or follow from PSI, and how dynamics of party competition and cooperation more broadly connect to mass polarization (e.g. Bassan-Nygate & Weiss, 2022).

---

[28] Similar dynamics may have been at play in Venezuela (e.g. Coppedge, 2005).

5.2 Political Behavior

If the effect of polarization on democracy is the foremost concern of scholars and pundits, its effect on democratic *attitudes* is likely a close second. Public support for democracy contributes to the resilience of democratic institutions (Claassen, 2020a), suggesting that democratic support could serve as a mediating variable between mass polarization and democracy itself. Many scholars purport to find support for this hypothesis, showing that polarization decreases citizens' support for democratic norms (Kingzette et al., 2021; Mason, 2018) and erodes their dedication to accountability (Finkel et al., 2020; Simonovits et al., 2022). Using experiments in the United States and Venezuela, Graham and Svolik demonstrate that voters are often presented with a tradeoff between upholding democracy and pursuing partisan goals and that individual voters' willingness to resolve this tradeoff at the expense of democracy increases as polities become more polarized (Graham & Svolik, 2020; Svolik, 2020).

However, some recent studies have pushed back on these findings. Broockman et al. (2023) show how results purportedly supporting the polarization-democratic support hypothesis are observationally equivalent to alternate explanations and find no evidence for the apparent connection between the two phenomena across five experiments. Voelkel et al. (2023) present two additional experiments with the same null findings and conclude that past work has substantially overestimated the existence of a causal link. Grossman et al. (2022) suggest, instead, that citizens simply value majoritarian democracy and view elected officials' actions as inherently democratic, even if they do not adhere to scholarly understandings of democracy. The dataset I present in this monograph, in concert with similar large-scale datasets of democratic support (Claassen, 2020b), may help disentangle this morass of conflicting evidence. Is the relationship between polarization and democratic support conditional on the quality of democracy experienced by citizens? Does it take different forms in countries with more or less majoritarian institutions? Could polarization, in fact, be causally downstream from level of democracy, thereby complicating the purported relationship between polarization and democratic support?

One of the hallmarks of a healthy democracy is that citizens participate in the democratic process, with voting being perhaps the most common form of participation. Does mass polarization enhance voter turnout or suppress it? Fiorina (2005) posits that polarization decreases turnout by making voters feel that they are not well-represented by the menu of electoral options. Abramowitz and Stone (2006) disagree, arguing that polarization energizes voters. In the 2000 and 2004 US presidential elections, they show citizens who were more ideologically extreme and had a wider gap in affect between the two major party candidates were more likely to vote and to engage in other forms of participation.

To what extent is this finding reflected in multiparty systems, which often offer a wider array of mainstream and radical parties? Moral (2017) shows that more severe party polarization is associated with higher turnout in European multiparty democracies, but the level of turnout remains unaffected by voters' *perceptions* of polarization, leaving questions about whether mass polarization would exhibit a similar effect. Schmitt and Freire (2012) uncover a possible source of effect heterogeneity, showing the correlation between turnout and ideological polarization is positive in consolidated democracies but negative in post-Communist states. Future work should further investigate similar sources of variation. With PolarCAP data, scholars may even be able to causally identify the effect of polarization on turnout – an important data point for assessing the overall impact of polarization on democracy.

Populism frequently appears alongside declining democratic support and is often discussed in tandem with mass polarization. Case studies in the United States (Abramowitz & McCoy, 2019), Greece (Andreadis & Stavrakakis, 2019), and Hungary (Enyedi, 2016) demonstrate how populism and polarization can co-occur and interact with each other, contributing to democratic malaise in some cases. Other authors are more explicit about the theoretical connection, positing that populist politicians almost always provoke mass polarization (Fomina & Kucharczyk, 2016; Handlin, 2018; Roberts, 2022). Yet the story is likely not so simple. Mudde and Rovira Kaltwasser (2018) point out a more complicated relationship between the two phenomena: Ideological convergence (i.e. low polarization) opens the door to populist parties, which can then spark polarization. To what extent is there a feedback loop between polarization and populism? Perhaps the story is more complicated still, and a period of polarization must precede ideological convergence in order for there to exist a sufficient vacuum for populist parties to fill (e.g. Ignazi, 1992). Highly dynamic processes such as this lend themselves well to the type of longitudinal data I provide in this volume, and the continued prominence of populist parties in many consolidated and fledgling democracies alike brings heightened urgency to these questions.

Other scholarly questions surrounding mass polarization are perhaps less urgent but speak more directly to foundational public opinion research. For instance, what is the relationship between elite and mass polarization? Citizens tend to follow their party leaders when it comes to forming opinions on issues of the day (Lenz, 2012), so it stands to reason that polarization among elites is likely to be reflected in their constituents. Tworzecki (2019) characterizes Poland as "a case of top-down polarization," Adams et al. (2012a) show the Dutch public followed their leaders by *depolarizing* in the late twentieth century, and Rogowski and Sutherland (2016) argue affective polarization is a response to elite ideological polarization.

On the other hand, Adams et al. (2012b) demonstrate that the elite-mass depolarization seen in the Netherlands does not extend to the United Kingdom, and Kongkirati (2024) portrays the polarization of Thailand as driven in large part by conflict among the masses. LeBas and Munemo (2019) use the case of Zimbabwe to suggest a possible scope condition: Polarization extends to the masses when elites successfully activate a cleavage relating to the purpose of the state in society and foundational myths of the nation (see also Mallen & García-Guadilla, 2017; Rahman, 2019). The answer to the question of how elite and mass polarization are related likely includes multiple scope conditions and moderating variables such as this one; examining mass polarization across a wide range of cases and identifying multiple episodes of polarization within the same case at different time points – as LeBas and Munemo (2019) do – may hold promise for identifying the conditions under which elites spark mass polarization and citizens drive polarization themselves.

The specific type of cleavages cited by LeBas and Munemo (2019), among others, also speak to a storied literature that is often invoked to explain how and when polarization occurs. In short, cleavage theory holds that politics is shaped in part by the social divisions present within a country (Lipset, 1960; Lipset & Rokkan, 1967). When these cleavages are cross-cutting, social conflict tends to be less severe and citizens tend to be more weakly tied to their preferred party (Campbell et al., 1960; Powell, 1976). If these cleavages align and begin to reinforce one another along a single dimension, however, polarization is said to become more severe (Mason, 2016). In fact, Nordlinger (1972, p. 93) proclaims, "the hypothesis that politically relevant divisions which cross-cut each other contribute to the mitigation and regulation of conflicts is probably the explanatory hypothesis most widely accepted among American political scientists."

But does this cleavage-based theory of polarization stand up to empirics? Caughey et al. (2018) provide evidence from the United States, showing that geographic cleavages have declined in importance and economic, racial, and social liberalism have become increasingly intertwined across partisan subconstituencies. Rahman (2019) shows how overlapping ethnolinguistic, religious, and political cleavages fueled polarization in Bangladesh, but is careful to note that elites needed to provided the spark for that fuel to ignite – the cleavage structure alone did not trigger polarization of its own accord. Conversely, Slater and Arugay (2018) argue that politicized social cleavages were not responsible for polarization in several Asian democracies, and indeed were barely present at all in the Philippines (Arugay & Slater, 2019). McCoy and Somer (2019) survey eleven case studies and conclude that although contentious, reinforcing social cleavages are often present, they are neither a necessary nor sufficient condition to produce mass polarization.

What, then, should we make of this prominent theoretical framework? One possibility might be that it is not so much the cleavage structure itself that lends itself to polarization, but rather the rapid socioeconomic changes that often accompany the reshaping of cleavages. Could the mixed evidence for the cleavage-based theory of polarization be a simple case of omitted variable bias? Emizet (1999) shows that economic development and democratization in Africa shape the extent to which social cleavages become politicized by introducing new patterns of corruption and access to informal markets. Similarly, Hooghe and Marks (2018) show that a new transnational cleavage in Europe is structured around reactions to European integration and immigration. These sociopolitical shocks also opened the door for radical right parties to enter the party system, capitalizing on the new cleavage and providing a source of polarizing rhetoric. Whatever mass polarization occurred in these cases may therefore be at least partially attributable to destabilizing macro-level changes, not necessarily the reshaped cleavages that resulted from them. Defining and measuring polarization independent of cleavages, as I do in this volume, enables scholars to test this hypothesis in multiple ways, including focused case studies and cross-national analyses.

5.3 Conclusion

As a wave of mass polarization continues to envelop both consolidated democracies and developing countries at the time of writing, understanding the precursors and possible consequences of this unique form of political conflict is perhaps as important as ever. In this section and the one preceding it, I briefly described the topics I view as some of the most theoretically and practically significant, but I barely scratched the surface of the broad range of possible directions scholars might take this research agenda. Does polarization diffuse across state lines, much like policy or democracy? How do ideological and affective polarization interact and contribute to one another? Do federal systems defuse political conflict or amplify it? Are ethnically diverse polities more prone to mass polarization? In this monograph, I have provided a resource for scholars to begin answering these questions with a level of granularity, generalizability, and causal attribution that previously has not been possible.

I make these data freely available for use. I recommend accessing PolarCAP data using the associated R package – PolarCAP: Access the Polarization in Comparative Attitudes Project – available on the Comprehensive R Archive Network (Mehlhaff, 2023). A companion website describes how to easily incorporate this data portal into existing data analysis pipelines (https://imehlhaff.net/PolarCAP). For users not familiar with R or who require the full data file, this website provides a variety of file formats available for download.

References

Abedi, A. (2002). Challenges to Established Parties: The Effects of Party System Features on the Electoral Fortunes of Anti-Political-Establishment Parties. *European Journal of Political Research, 41*(4), 551–583.

Abramowitz, A., & McCoy, J. (2019). United States: Racial Resentment, Negative Partisanship, and Polarization in Trump's America. *The ANNALS of the American Academy of Political and Social Science, 681*(1), 137–156.

Abramowitz, A. I., & Saunders, K. L. (2008). Is Polarization a Myth? *The Journal of Politics, 70*(2), 542–555.

Abramowitz, A. I., & Stone, W. J. (2006). The Bush Effect: Polarization, Turnout, and Activism in the 2004 Presidential Election. *Presidential Studies Quarterly, 36*(2), 141–154.

Abramowitz, A. I., & Webster, S. (2016). The Rise of Negative Partisanship and the Nationalization of U.S. Elections in the 21st Century. *Electoral Studies, 41*, 12–22.

Acemoglu, D., & Robinson, J. A. (2006). *Economic Origins of Dictatorship and Democracy*. Cambridge University Press.

Adams, J., Bracken, D., Gidron, N. et al. (2023). Can't We All Just Get Along? How Women MPs Can Ameliorate Affective Polarization in Western Publics. *American Political Science Review, 117*(1), 318–324.

Adams, J., De Vries, C. E., & Leiter, D. (2012a). Subconstituency Reactions to Elite Depolarization in the Netherlands: An Analysis of the Dutch Public's Policy Beliefs and Partisan Loyalties, 1986–98. *British Journal of Political Science, 42*(1), 81–105.

Adams, J., Ezrow, L., & Wlezien, C. (2016). The Company You Keep: How Voters Infer Party Positions on European Integration from Governing Coalition Arrangements. *American Journal of Political Science, 60*(4), 811–823.

Adams, J., Green, J., & Milazzo, C. (2012b). Has the British Public Depolarized along with Political Elites? An American Perspective on British Public Opinion. *Comparative Political Studies, 45*(4), 507–530.

Adida, C. L., Ferree, K. E., Posner, D. N., & Robinson, A. L. (2016). Who's Asking? Interviewer Coethnicity Effects in African Survey Data. *Comparative Political Studies, 49*(12), 1630–1660.

Ahler, D. J., & Broockman, D. E. (2018). The Delegate Paradox: Why Polarized Politicians Can Represent Citizens Best. *The Journal of Politics, 80*(4), 1117–1133.

References

Ahler, D. J., & Sood, G. (2018). The Parties in Our Heads: Misperceptions about Party Composition and Their Consequences. *The Journal of Politics, 80*(3), 964–981.

Aldrich, J. H., & Rohde, D. W. (2000). The Republican Revolution and the House Appropriations Committee. *The Journal of Politics, 62*(1), 1–33.

Algara, C., & Zur, R. (2023). The Downsian Roots of Affective Polarization. *Electoral Studies, 82*, 102581.

Anderson, M. D. (2011). *Disaster Writing: The Cultural Politics of Catastrophe in Latin America*. University of Virginia Press.

Andreadis, I., & Stavrakakis, Y. (2019). Dynamics of Polarization in the Greek Case. *The ANNALS of the American Academy of Political and Social Science, 681*(1), 157–172.

Ansolabehere, S., & Iyengar, S. (1995). *Going Negative: How Political Advertisements Shrink and Polarize the Electorate*. The Free Press.

Ares, M., Bürgisser, R., & Häusermann, S. (2021). Attitudinal Polarization towards the Redistributive Role of the State in the Wake of the COVID-19 Crisis. *Journal of Elections, Public Opinion and Parties, 31*, 41–55.

Ariely, G., & Davidov, E. (2012). Assessment of Measurement Equivalence with Cross-National and Longitudinal Surveys in Political Science. *European Political Science, 11*(3), 363–377.

Arugay, A. A., & Slater, D. (2019). Polarization without Poles: Machiavellian Conflicts and the Philippines' Lost Decade of Democracy, 2000–2010. *The ANNALS of the American Academy of Political and Social Science, 681*(1), 122–136.

Bale, T., & Rovira Kaltwasser, C. (Eds.). (2021). *Riding the Populist Wave: Europe's Mainstream Right in Crisis*. Cambridge University Press.

Barber, M. J., & McCarty, N. (2015). Causes and Consequences of Polarization. In N. Persily (Ed.), *Solutions to Political Polarization in America* (pp. 15–58). Cambridge University Press.

Barnes, W. A. (1998). Incomplete Democracy in Central America: Polarization and Voter Turnout in Nicaragua and El Salvador. *Journal of Interamerican Studies and World Affairs, 40*(3), 63–101.

Bassan-Nygate, L., & Weiss, C. M. (2022). Party Competition and Cooperation Shape Affective Polarization: Evidence from Natural and Survey Experiments in Israel. *Comparative Political Studies, 55*(2), 287–318.

Beck, N. (1989). Estimating Dynamic Models Using Kalman Filtering. *Political Analysis, 1*, 121–156.

Beinart, W. (2001). *Twentieth-Century South Africa*. Oxford University Press.

Bell, D. S. (2018). *Parties and Democracy in France: Parties under Presidentialism*. Routledge.

Bermeo, N. (2003). *Ordinary People in Extraordinary Times: The Citizenry and the Breakdown of Democracy*. Princeton University Press.

Binder, S. A. (1999). The Dynamics of Legislative Gridlock, 1947–96. *American Political Science Review, 93*(3), 519–533.

Bischof, D., & Wagner, M. (2019). Do Voters Polarize When Radical Parties Enter Parliament? *American Journal of Political Science, 63*(4), 888–904.

Blakeley, G. (2006). "It's Politics, Stupid!" The Spanish General Election of 2004. *Parliamentary Affairs, 59*(2), 331–349.

Bonica, A., McCarty, N., Poole, K. T., & Rosenthal, H. (2015). Congressional Polarization and Its Connection to Income Inequality: An Update. In J. A. Thurber & A. Yoshinaka (Eds.), *American Gridlock: The Sources, Character, and Impact of Political Polarization* (pp. 357–377). Cambridge University Press.

Bornschier, S. (2019). Historical Polarization and Representation in South American Party Systems, 1900–1990. *British Journal of Political Science, 49*(1), 153–179.

Bowman, K. (2008). *America and the War on Terrorism*. American Enterprise Institute. Washington, DC. www.aei.org/wp-content/uploads/2011/10/20050805_terror0805.pdf?x91208.

Boxell, L., Gentzkow, M., & Shapiro, J. M. (2024). Cross-Country Trends in Affective Polarization. *Review of Economics and Statistics, 106*(2), 557–565.

Bratton, M., & van de Walle, N. (1997). *Democratic Experiments in Africa: Regime Transitions in Comparative Perspective*. Cambridge University Press.

Broockman, D. E., Kalla, J. L., & Westwood, S. J. (2023). Does Affective Polarization Undermine Democratic Norms or Accountability? Maybe Not. *American Journal of Political Science 67*(3), 808–828.

Bruhn, K. (1997). *Taking on Goliath: The Emergence of a New Left Party and the Struggle for Democracy in Mexico*. The Pennsylvania State University Press.

Bruhn, K., & Greene, K. F. (2007). Elite Polarization Meets Mass Moderation in Mexico's 2006 Elections. *PS: Political Science & Politics, 40*(1), 33–38.

Bünte, M., & Thompson, M. R. (2023). Presidentialism and Democracy in East and Southeast Asia: Between Resilience and Regression. In M. Bünte & M. R. Thompson (Eds.), *Presidentialism and Democracy in East and Southeast Asia* (pp. 1–19). Routledge.

Campbell, A., Converse, P. E., Miller, W. E., & Stokes, D. E. (1960). *The American Voter*. The University of Chicago Press.

Canes-Wrone, B., & Park, J.-K. (2012). Electoral Business Cycles in OECD Countries. *American Political Science Review, 106*(1), 103–122.

Carlin, R. E., Love, G. J., & Martínez-Gallardo, C. (2015). Cushioning the Fall: Scandals, Economic Conditions, and Executive Approval. *Political Behavior, 37*(1), 109–130.

Caughey, D., Dunham, J., & Warshaw, C. (2018). The Ideological Nationalization of Partisan Subconstituencies in the American States. *Public Choice, 176*(1–2), 133–151.

Caughey, D., O'Grady, T., & Warshaw, C. (2019). Policy Ideology in European Mass Publics, 1981–2016. *American Political Science Review, 113*(3), 674–693.

Caughey, D., & Warshaw, C. (2015). Dynamic Estimation of Latent Opinion Using a Hierarchical Group-Level IRT Model. *Political Analysis, 23*(2), 197–211.

Chari, R. (2004). The 2004 Spanish Election: Terrorism as a Catalyst for Change? *West European Politics, 27*(5), 954–963.

Chari, R. S. (2000). The March 2000 Spanish Election: A "Critical Election?" *West European Politics, 23*(3), 207–214.

Chávez, J. M. (2017). *Poets and Prophets of the Resistance: Intellectuals and the Origins of El Salvador's Civil War*. Oxford University Press.

Cheibub, J. A., Przeworski, A., & Saiegh, S. M. (2004). Government Coalitions and Legislative Success under Presidentialism and Parliamentarism. *British Journal of Political Science, 34*(4), 565–587.

Claassen, C. (2019). Estimating Smooth Country–Year Panels of Public Opinion. *Political Analysis, 27*(1), 1–20.

Claassen, C. (2020a). Does Public Support Help Democracy Survive? *American Journal of Political Science, 64*(1), 118–134.

Claassen, C. (2020b). In the Mood for Democracy? Democratic Support as Thermostatic Opinion. *American Political Science Review, 114*(1), 36–53.

Conlan, T. J., & Posner, P. L. (2016). American Federalism in an Era of Partisan Polarization: The Intergovernmental Paradox of Obama's "New Nationalism." *Publius: The Journal of Federalism, 46*(3), 281–307.

Converse, P. E. (1964). The Nature of Belief Systems in Mass Publics. In D. E. Apter (Ed.), *Ideology and Discontent* (pp. 206–261). The Free Press of Glencoe.

Coppedge, M. (2005). Explaining Democratic Deterioration in Venezuela through Nested Inference. In F. Hagopian & S. P. Mainwaring (Eds.), *The Third Wave of Democratization in Latin America: Advances and Setbacks* (pp. 289–316). Cambridge University Press.

Coppedge, M., Gerring, J., Knutsen, C. H. et al. (2020). *V-Dem Country-Year: V-Dem Core Dataset v10*. Varieties of Democracy (V-Dem) Project. Gothenburg, Sweden.

Cox, G. W. (1990). Centripetal and Centrifugal Incentives in Electoral Systems. *American Journal of Political Science, 34*(4), 903–935.

Cruz, C., Keefer, P., & Scartascini, C. (2021). *Database of Political Institutions*. Inter-American Development Bank Research Department. Washington, DC.

Curini, L., & Hino, A. (2012). Missing Links in Party-System Polarization: How Institutions and Voters Matter. *The Journal of Politics, 74*(2), 460–473.

Dalpino, C. (2011). Thailand in 2010: Rupture and Attempts at Reconciliation. *Asian Survey, 51*(1), 155–162.

Dalton, R. J. (2008). The Quantity and the Quality of Party Systems: Party System Polarization, Its Measurement, and Its Consequences. *Comparative Political Studies, 41*(7), 899–920.

Dalton, R. J., & Wattenberg, M. P. (Eds.). (2000). *Parties without Partisans: Political Change in Advanced Industrial Democracies*. Oxford University Press.

de Ayala, R. J. (2022). *The Theory and Practice of Item Response Theory* (2nd ed.). Guilford Press.

Dibble, S. (2014). 1994 Assassination Still Resonates in Mexico [newspaper]. *The San Diego Union-Tribune*. www.sandiegouniontribune.com/news/border-baja-california/sdut-tijuana-colosio-lomas-taurinas-pri-mexico-politics-2014mar22-story.html

DiMaggio, P., Evans, J., & Bryson, B. (1996). Have American's Social Attitudes Become More Polarized? *American Journal of Sociology, 102*(3), 690–755.

Dow, J. K. (2011). Party-System Extremism in Majoritarian and Proportional Electoral Systems. *British Journal of Political Science, 41*(2), 341–361.

Down, I., & Wilson, C. J. (2008). From "Permissive Consensus" to "Constraining Dissensus": A Polarizing Union? *Acta Politica, 43*(1), 26–49.

Downs, A. (1957). *An Economic Theory of Democracy*. Harper & Brothers.

Drutman, L. (2020). *Breaking the Two-Party Doom Loop: The Case for Multiparty Democracy in America*. Oxford University Press.

Duverger, M. (1954). *Political Parties: Their Organization and Activity in the Modern State* (B. North & R. North, Trans.). Wiley.

Emizet, K. N. (1999). Political Cleavages in a Democratizing Society: The Case of the Congo (Formerly Zaire). *Comparative Political Studies, 32*(2), 185–228.

Encarnación, O. G. (2008). *Spanish Politics: Democracy after Dictatorship*. Polity Press.

Enyedi, Z. (2016). Populist Polarization and Party System Institutionalization: The Role of Party Politics in De-Democratization. *Problems of Post-Communism, 63*(4), 210–220.

Erikson, R. S., MacKuen, M. B., & Stimson, J. A. (2002). *The Macro Polity.* Cambridge University Press.

Esteban, J.-M., & Ray, D. (1994). On the Measurement of Polarization. *Econometrica, 62*(4), 819–851.

Ezrow, L. (2008). Parties' Policy Programmes and the Dog that Didn't Bark: No Evidence that Proportional Systems Promote Extreme Party Positioning. *British Journal of Political Science, 38*(3), 479–497.

Ezrow, L. (2011). Reply to Dow: Party Positions, Votes and the Mediating Role of Electoral Systems? *British Journal of Political Science, 41*(2), 448–452.

Ezrow, L., Tavits, M., & Homola, J. (2014). Voter Polarization, Strength of Partisanship, and Support for Extremist Parties. *Comparative Political Studies, 47*(11), 1558–1583.

Faundez, J. (1997). In Defense of Presidentialism: The Case of Chile, 1932–1970. In S. Mainwaring & M. S. Shugart (Eds.), *Presidentialism and Democracy in Latin America* (pp. 300–320). Cambridge University Press.

Finkel, E. J., Bail, C. A., Cikara, M. et al. (2020). Political Sectarianism in America. *Science, 370*(6516), 533–536.

Fiorina, M. P. (2005). *Culture War? The Myth of a Polarized America.* Pearson Longman.

Fomina, J., & Kucharczyk, J. (2016). Populism and Protest in Poland. *Journal of Democracy, 27*(4), 58–68.

Fortunato, D. (2021). *The Cycle of Coalition: How Parties and Voters Interact under Coalition Governance.* Cambridge University Press.

Fortunato, D., & Stevenson, R. T. (2013). Perceptions of Partisan Ideologies: The Effect of Coalition Participation. *American Journal of Political Science, 57*(2), 459–477.

Fortunato, D., & Stevenson, R. T. (2021). Party Government and Political Information. *Legislative Studies Quarterly, 46*(2), 251–295.

Fowler, A., Hill, S. J., Lewis, J. B. et al. (2023). Moderates. *American Political Science Review, 117*(2), 643–660.

Funke, M., Schularick, M., & Trebesch, C. (2016). Going to Extremes: Politics after Financial Crises, 1870–2014. *European Economic Review, 88*, 227–260.

Garry, J. (2007). Making "Party Identification" More Versatile: Operationalising the Concept for the Multiparty Setting. *Electoral Studies, 26*(2), 346–358.

Garzia, D., Ferreira da Silva, F., & Maye, S. (2023). Affective Polarization in Comparative and Longitudinal Perspective. *Public Opinion Quarterly, 87*(1), 219–231.

Gelman, A. (2009). *Red State, Blue State, Rich State, Poor State: Why Americans Vote the Way They Do* (2nd ed.). Princeton University Press.

Gelman, A., & Hill, J. (2007). *Data Analysis Using Regression and Multilevel/Hierarchical Models*. Cambridge University Press.

Gibson, J. L. (2004). *Overcoming Apartheid: Can Truth Reconcile a Divided Nation?* Russell Sage Foundation.

Gidron, N., Adams, J., & Horne, W. (2020). *American Affective Polarization in Comparative Perspective*. Cambridge University Press.

Gidron, N., Adams, J., & Horne, W. (2023). Who Dislikes Whom? Affective Polarization between Pairs of Parties in Western Democracies. *British Journal of Political Science, 53*(3), 997–1015.

Gidron, N., Sheffer, L., & Mor, G. (2022). Validating the Feeling Thermometer as a Measure of Partisan Affect in Multi-Party Systems. *Electoral Studies, 80*, 102542.

Golub, S. S. (1991). The Political Economy of the Latin American Debt Crisis. *Latin American Research Review, 26*(1), 175–215.

Goplerud, M. (2019). A Multinomial Framework for Ideal Point Estimation. *Political Analysis, 27*(1), 69–89.

Graham, M., & Svolik, M. W. (2020). Democracy in America? Partisanship, Polarization, and the Robustness of Support for Democracy in the United States. *American Political Science Review, 114*(2), 392–409.

Grechyna, D. (2016). On the Determinants of Political Polarization. *Economics Letters, 144*, 10–14.

Green, J., & Jennings, W. (2012). Valence as Macro-Competence: An Analysis of Mood in Party Competence Evaluations in Great Britain. *British Journal of Political Science, 42*(2), 311–343.

Groenendyk, E., Sances, M. W., & Zhirkov, K. (2020). Intraparty Polarization in American Politics. *The Journal of Politics, 82*(4), 1616–1620.

Großer, J., & Palfrey, T. R. (2019). Candidate Entry and Political Polarization: An Experimental Study. *American Political Science Review, 113*(1), 209–225.

Grossman, G., Kronick, D., Levendusky, M., & Meredith, M. (2022). The Majoritarian Threat to Liberal Democracy. *Journal of Experimental Political Science, 9*, 36–45.

Guinote, A., & Fiske, S. T. (2003). Being in the Outgroup Territory Increases Stereotypic Perceptions of Outgroups: Situational Sources of Category Activation. *Group Processes & Intergroup Relations, 6*(4), 323–331.

References

Gunderson, J. R. (2022). When Does Income Inequality Cause Polarization? *British Journal of Political Science, 52*(3), 1315–1332.

Handlin, S. (2017). *State Crisis in Fragile Democracies: Polarization and Political Regimes in South America*. Cambridge University Press.

Handlin, S. (2018). The Logic of Polarizing Populism: State Crises and Polarization in South America. *American Behavioral Scientist, 62*(1), 75–91.

Hare, C., Armstrong II, D. A., Bakker, R., Carroll, R., & Poole, K. T. (2015). Using Bayesian Aldrich-McKelvey Scaling to Study Citizens' Ideological Preferences and Perceptions. *American Journal of Political Science, 59*(3), 759–774.

Hebenstreit, J. (2022). Voter Polarisation in Germany: Unpolarised Western but Polarised Eastern Germany? *German Politics 32*(1), 63–84.

Hetherington, M. J. (2001). Resurgent Mass Partisanship: The Role of Elite Polarization. *American Political Science Review, 95*(3), 619–631.

Hetherington, M. J. (2009). Putting Polarization in Perspective. *British Journal of Political Science, 39*(2), 413–448.

Heywood, P. M. (2003). Desperately Seeking Influence: Spain and the War in Iraq. *European Political Science, 3*(1), 35–40.

Hill, S. J., & Tausanovitch, C. (2015). A Disconnect in Representation? Comparison of Trends in Congressional and Public Polarization. *The Journal of Politics, 77*(4), 1058–1075.

Hobolt, S. B., & Tilley, J. (2016). Fleeing the Centre: The Rise of Challenger Parties in the Aftermath of the Euro Crisis. *West European Politics, 39*(5), 971–991.

Hooghe, L., & Marks, G. (2018). Cleavage Theory Meets Europe's Crises: Lipset, Rokkan, and the Transnational Cleavage. *Journal of European Public Policy, 25*(1), 109–135.

Horne, W., Adams, J., & Gidron, N. (2023). The Way We Were: How Histories of Co-Governance Alleviate Partisan Hostility. *Comparative Political Studies, 56*(3), 299–325.

Horowitz, D. L. (1990). Comparing Democratic Systems. *Journal of Democracy, 1*(4), 73–79.

Huber, E., & Stephens, J. D. (2001). *Development and Crisis of the Welfare State: Parties and Politics in Global Markets*. The University of Chicago Press.

Huber, E., & Stephens, J. D. (2012). *Democracy and the Left: Social Policy and Inequality in Latin America*. The University of Chicago Press.

Huddy, L. (2001). From Social to Political Identity: A Critical Examination of Social Identity Theory. *Political Psychology, 22*(1), 127–156. www.jstor.org/stable/3791909.

Human Rights Watch. (2011). *Descent into Chaos: Thailand's 2010 Red Shirt Protests and the Government Crackdown.* www.hrw.org/report/2011/05/03/descent-chaos/thailands-2010-red-shirt-protests-and-government-crackdown.

Huntington, S. P. (1968). *Political Order in Changing Societies.* Yale University Press.

Ignazi, P. (1992). The Silent Counter-Revolution: Hypotheses on the Emergence of Extreme Right-Wing Parties in Europe. *European Journal of Political Research, 22*(1), 3–34.

Imai, K. (2011). Introduction to the Virtual Issue: Past and Future Research Agenda on Causal Inference. *Political Analysis, 19*(V2), 1–4.

Ishiyama, J. T., & Velten, M. (1998). Presidential Power and Democratic Development in Post-Communist Politics. *Communist and Post-Communist Studies, 31*(3), 217–233.

Iversen, T., & Soskice, D. (2015). Information, Inequality, and Mass Polarization: Ideology in Advanced Democracies. *Comparative Political Studies, 48*(13), 1781–1813.

Iyengar, S., Sood, G., & Lelkes, Y. (2012). Affect, Not Ideology: A Social Identity Perspective on Polarization. *Public Opinion Quarterly, 76*(3), 405–431.

Jackman, S. (2005). Pooling the Polls over an Election Campaign. *Australian Journal of Political Science, 40*(4), 499–517.

Jensen, C., & Thomsen, J. P. F. (2013). Can Party Competition Amplify Mass Ideological Polarization over Public Policy? The Case of Ethnic Exclusionism in Denmark and Sweden. *Party Politics, 19*(5), 821–840.

Jiménez, F. (2004). The Politics of Scandal in Spain: Morality Plays, Social Trust, and the Battle for Public Opinion. *American Behavioral Scientist, 47*(8), 1099–1121.

Kekkonen, A., & Ylä-Anttila, T. (2021). Affective Blocs: Understanding Affective Polarization in Multiparty Systems. *Electoral Studies, 72*, 102367.

Kernell, S., & Rice, L. L. (2011). Cable and the Partisan Polarization of the President's Audience. *Presidential Studies Quarterly, 41*(4), 693–711.

King, G., Keohane, R. O., & Verba, S. (1994). *Designing Social Inquiry: Scientific Inference in Qualitative Research.* Princeton University Press.

Kingzette, J., Druckman, J. N., Klar, S. et al. (2021). How Affective Polarization Undermines Support for Democratic Norms. *Public Opinion Quarterly, 85*(2), 663–677.

Klesner, J. L. (2007). The 2006 Mexican Elections: Manifestation of a Divided Society? *PS: Political Science & Politics, 40*(1), 27–32.

Kongkirati, P. (2024). *Thailand: Contestation, Polarization, and Democratic Regression.* Cambridge University Press.

Lambert, A. J., Schott, J. P., & Scherer, L. (2011). Threat, Politics, and Attitudes: Toward a Greater Understanding of Rally-'Round-the-Flag Effects. *Current Directions in Psychological Science, 20*(6), 343–348.

LeBas, A., & Munemo, N. (2019). Elite Conflict, Compromise, and Enduring Authoritarianism: Polarization in Zimbabwe, 1980–2008. *The ANNALS of the American Academy of Political and Social Science, 681*(1), 209–226.

Lee, F. E. (2016). *Insecure Majorities: Congress and the Perpetual Campaign*. The University of Chicago Press.

Lelkes, Y. (2016). Mass Polarization: Manifestations and Measurements. *Public Opinion Quarterly, 80*(S1), 392–410.

Lelkes, Y., & Westwood, S. J. (2017). The Limits of Partisan Prejudice. *The Journal of Politics, 79*(2), 485–501.

Lenz, G. S. (2012). *Follow the Leader? How Voters Respond to Politicians' Policies and Performance*. The University of Chicago Press.

Levendusky, M. (2009). *The Partisan Sort: How Liberals Became Democrats and Conservatives Became Republicans*. University of Chicago Press.

Levendusky, M. S., & Pope, J. C. (2011). Red States vs. Blue States: Going beyond the Mean. *Public Opinion Quarterly, 75*(2), 227–248.

Lieberman, R. C., Mettler, S., Pepinsky, T. B., Roberts, K. M., & Valelly, R. (2019). The Trump Presidency and American Democracy: A Historical and Comparative Analysis. *Perspectives on Politics, 17*(02), 470–479.

Lijphart, A. (1984). *Democracies: Patterns of Majoritarian and Consensus Government Twenty-one Countries*. Yale University Press.

Lijphart, A. (1994). *Electoral Systems and Party Systems: A Study of Twenty-Seven Democracies, 1945–1990*. Oxford University Press.

Lindqvist, E., & Östling, R. (2010). Political Polarization and the Size of Government. *American Political Science Review, 104*(3), 543–565.

Linz, J. J. (1978). *The Breakdown of Democratic Regimes: Crisis, Breakdown, and Reequilibration* (J. J. Linz & A. Stepan, Eds.; Vol. 1). The Johns Hopkins University Press.

Linz, J. J. (1990). The Perils of Presidentialism. *Journal of Democracy, 1*(1), 51–69.

Linzer, D. A. (2013). Dynamic Bayesian Forecasting of Presidential Elections in the States. *Journal of the American Statistical Association, 108*(501), 124–134.

Lipset, S. M. (1960). *Political Man: The Social Bases of Politics*. Doubleday.

Lipset, S. M., & Rokkan, S. (1967). Cleavage Structures, Party Systems, and Voter Alignments: An Introduction. In S. M. Lipset & S. Rokkan (Eds.), *Party Systems and Voter Alignments: Cross-National Perspectives* (pp. 1–64). The Free Press.

López, E. J., & Ramírez, C. D. (2004). Party Polarization and the Business Cycle in the United States. *Public Choice, 121*(3–4), 413–430.

Lowande, K., & Rogowski, J. C. (2021). Executive Power in Crisis. *American Political Science Review, 115*(4), 1406–1423.

Lowande, K. S., & Milkis, S. M. (2014). "We Can't Wait": Barack Obama, Partisan Polarization and the Administrative Presidency. *The Forum, 12*(1), 3–27.

Lührmann, A., & Lindberg, S. I. (2019). A Third Wave of Autocratization is Here: What is New about It? *Democratization, 26*(7), 1095–1113.

Lupu, N. (2016). *Party Brands in Crisis: Partisanship, Brand Dilution, and the Breakdown of Political Parties in Latin America*. Cambridge University Press.

Mainwaring, S. (1993). Presidentialism, Multipartism, and Democracy: The Difficult Combination. *Comparative Political Studies, 26*(2), 198–228.

Mainwaring, S., & Bizzarro, F. (2018). Democratization without Party System Institutionalization: Cross-National Correlates. In S. Mainwaring (Ed.), *Party Systems in Latin America: Institutionalization, Decay, and Collapse* (pp. 102–132). Cambridge University Press.

Mallen, A. L., & García-Guadilla, M. P. (2017). *Venezuela's Polarized Politics: The Paradox of Direct Democracy under Chávez*. First Forum Press.

Martín-Baró, I. (1989). Political Violence and War as Causes of Psychosocial Trauma in El Salvador. *International Journal of Mental Health, 18*(1), 3–20.

Mason, L. (2016). A Cross-Cutting Calm: How Social Sorting Drives Affective Polarization. *Public Opinion Quarterly, 80*(S1), 351–377.

Mason, L. (2018). *Uncivil Agreement: How Politics Became Our Identity*. The University of Chicago Press.

Matakos, K., Troumpounis, O., & Xefteris, D. (2016). Electoral Rule Disproportionality and Platform Polarization. *American Journal of Political Science, 60*(4), 1026–1043.

McCarty, N., Poole, K. T., & Rosenthal, H. (2006). *Polarized America: The Dance of Ideology and Unequal Riches* (2nd ed.). The MIT Press.

McCarty, N., Poole, K. T., & Rosenthal, H. (2009). Does Gerrymandering Cause Polarization? *American Journal of Political Science, 53*(3), 666–680.

McCoy, J., Rahman, T., & Somer, M. (2018). Polarization and the Global Crisis of Democracy: Common Patterns, Dynamics, and Pernicious Consequences for Democratic Polities. *American Behavioral Scientist, 62*(1), 16–42.

McCoy, J., & Somer, M. (2019). Toward a Theory of Pernicious Polarization and How It Harms Democracies: Comparative Evidence and Possible Remedies. *The ANNALS of the American Academy of Political and Social Science, 681*(1), 234–271.

McCoy, J. L., & McConnell, S. A. (1997). Nicaragua: Beyond the Revolution. *Current History, 96*(607), 75–80.

McCullagh, C. B. (2000). Bias in Historical Description, Interpretation, and Explanation. *History and Theory, 39*(1), 39–66.

McDonald, M. D., Mendes, S. M., & Kim, M. (2007). Cross-Temporal and Cross-National Comparisons of Party Left-Right Positions. *Electoral Studies, 26*(1), 62–75.

McGraw, K. O., & Wong, S. P. (1996). Forming Inferences about Some Intraclass Correlation Coefficients. *Psychological Methods, 1*(1), 30–46.

Mehlhaff, I. D. (2023). *PolarCAP: Access the Polarization in Comparative Attitudes Project.* Comprehensive R Archive Network. https://cran.r-project.org/package=PolarCAP.

Mehlhaff, I. D. (2024). A Group-Based Approach to Measuring Polarization. *American Political Science Review, 118*(3), 1518–1526.

Meltzer, A. H., & Richard, S. F. (1981). A Rational Theory of the Size of Government. *Journal of Political Economy, 89*(5), 914–927.

Miller, L. (2020). *Polarización en España: Más divididos por ideología e identidad que por políticas públicas* (EsadeEcPol Insight 18). Center for Economic Policy and Political Economy.

Moral, M. (2017). The Bipolar Voter: On the Effects of Actual and Perceived Party Polarization on Voter Turnout in European Multiparty Democracies. *Political Behavior, 39*(4), 935–965.

Mudde, C., & Rovira Kaltwasser, C. (2017). *Populism: A Very Short Introduction.* Oxford University Press.

Mudde, C., & Rovira Kaltwasser, C. (2018). Studying Populism in Comparative Perspective: Reflections on the Contemporary and Future Research Agenda. *Comparative Political Studies, 51*(13), 1667–1693.

Munger, K., Guess, A. M., & Hargittai, E. (2021). Quantitative Description of Digital Media: A Modest Proposal to Disrupt Academic Publishing. *Journal of Quantitative Description: Digital Media, 1*(1), 1–13.

Nall, C. (2018). *The Road to Inequality: How the Federal Highway Program Polarized America and Undermined Cities.* Cambridge University Press.

Newport, F. (2003). *Seventy-Two Percent of Americans Support War against Iraq.* Gallup. https://news.gallup.com/poll/8038/seventytwo-percent-americans-support-war-against-iraq.aspx.

Nordlinger, E. (1972). *Conflict Regulation in Divided Societies.* Harvard University Press.

O'Donnell, G., & Schmitter, P. C. (Eds.). (1986). *Transitions from Authoritarian Rule: Tentative Conclusions about Uncertain Democracies* (Vol. 4). The Johns Hopkins University Press.

Orhan, Y. E. (2022). The Relationship between Affective Polarization and Democratic Backsliding: Comparative Evidence. *Democratization, 29*(4), 714–735.

Park, B., & Judd, C. M. (1990). Measures and Models of Perceived Group Variability. *Journal of Personality and Social Psychology, 59*(2), 173–191.

Parsons, B. M. (2015). The Social Identity Politics of Peer Networks. *American Politics Research, 43*(4), 680–707.

Persily, N. (Ed.). (2015). *Solutions to Political Polarization in America*. Cambridge University Press.

Pontusson, J., & Rueda, D. (2008). Inequality as a Source of Political Polarization: A Comparative Analysis of Twelve OECD Countries. In P. Beramendi & C. J. Anderson (Eds.), *Democracy, Inequality, and Representation in Comparative Perspective* (pp. 312–353). Russell Sage Foundation.

Poole, K. T., & Rosenthal, H. (2001). D-Nominate after 10 Years: A Comparative Update to Congress: A Political-Economic History of Roll-Call Voting. *Legislative Studies Quarterly, 26*(1), 5–29.

Pop-Eleches, G., & Tucker, J. A. (2017). *Communism's Shadow: Historical Legacies and Contemporary Political Attitudes*. Princeton University Press.

Powell, G. B. (1976). Political Cleavage Structure, Cross-Pressure Processes, and Partisanship: An Empirical Test of the Theory. *American Journal of Political Science, 20*(1), 1–23.

Power, S. A., Madsen, T., & Morton, T. A. (2020). Relative Deprivation and Revolt: Current and Future Directions. *Current Opinion in Psychology, 35*, 119–124.

Power, T. J., & Gasiorowski, M. J. (1997). Institutional Design and Democratic Consolidation in the Third World. *Comparative Political Studies, 30*(2), 123–155.

Rahman, T. (2019). Party System Institutionalization and Pernicious Polarization in Bangladesh. *The ANNALS of the American Academy of Political and Social Science, 681*(1), 173–192.

Reckase, M. D. (2009). *Multidimensional Item Response Theory*. Springer.

Reeves, A., & Rogowski, J. C. (2022). *No Blank Check: The Origins and Consequences of Public Antipathy towards Presidential Power*. Cambridge University Press.

Rehm, P. (2011). Risk Inequality and the Polarized American Electorate. *British Journal of Political Science, 41*(2), 363–387.

Rehm, P., & Reilly, T. (2010). United We Stand: Constituency Homogeneity and Comparative Party Polarization. *Electoral Studies, 29*(1), 40–53.

Reiljan, A. (2020). "Fear and Loathing across Party Lines" (also) in Europe: Affective Polarisation in European Party Systems. *European Journal of Political Research, 59*(2), 376–396.

Reiljan, A., Garzia, D., Ferreira Da Silva, F., & Trechsel, A. H. (2024). Patterns of Affective Polarization toward Parties and Leaders across the Democratic World. *American Political Science Review, 118*(2), 654–670.

Roberts, K. M. (2022). Populism and Polarization in Comparative Perspective: Constitutive, Spatial and Institutional Dimensions. *Government and Opposition, 57*(4), 680–702.

Rogowski, J. C., & Sutherland, J. L. (2016). How Ideology Fuels Affective Polarization. *Political Behavior, 38*(2), 485–508.

Rosenfeld, S. (2018). *The Polarizers: Postwar Architects of Our Partisan Era*. The University of Chicago Press.

Rustow, D. A. (1970). Transitions to Democracy: Toward a Dynamic Model. *Comparative Politics, 2*(3), 337–363.

Samuels, D. J., & Zucco, C. (2018). *Partisans, Antipartisans, and Nonpartisans: Voting Behavior in Brazil*. Cambridge University Press.

Sartori, G. (1976). *Parties and Party Systems: A Framework for Analysis*. Cambridge University Press.

Schmitt, H., & Freire, A. (2012). Ideological Polarization: Different Worlds in East and West. In D. Sanders, P. Magalhães, & G. Toka (Eds.), *Citizens and the European Polity: Mass Attitudes towards the European and National Polities* (pp. 65–87). Oxford University Press.

Shugart, M. S., & Carey, J. M. (1992). *Presidents and Assemblies: Constitutional Design and Electoral Dynamics*. Cambridge University Press.

Sigelman, L., & Yough, S. N. (1978). Left-Right Polarization in National Party Systems: A Cross-National Analysis. *Comparative Political Studies, 11*(3), 355–379.

Simonovits, G., McCoy, J., & Littvay, L. (2022). Democratic Hypocrisy and Out-Group Threat: Explaining Citizen Support for Democratic Erosion. *The Journal of Politics, 84*(3), 1806–1811.

Singer, M. (2016). Elite Polarization and the Electoral Impact of Left-Right Placements: Evidence from Latin America, 1995–2009. *Latin American Research Review, 51*(2), 174–194.

Sisk, T. D. (1989). White Politics in South Africa: Polarization under Pressure. *Africa Today, 36*(1), 29–39.

Slater, D., & Arugay, A. A. (2018). Polarizing Figures: Executive Power and Institutional Conflict in Asian Democracies. *American Behavioral Scientist, 62*(1), 92–106.

Solt, F. (2020a). Measuring Income Inequality across Countries and over Time: The Standardized World Income Inequality Database. *Social Science Quarterly, 101*(3), 1183–1199.

Solt, F. (2020b). *Modeling Dynamic Comparative Public Opinion.* Pre-Print.

Somer, M. (2019). Turkey: The Slippery Slope from Reformist to Revolutionary Polarization and Democratic Breakdown. *The ANNALS of the American Academy of Political and Social Science, 681*(1), 42–61.

Southall, R. (2014). Democracy at Risk? Politics and Governance under the ANC. *The ANNALS of the American Academy of Political and Social Science, 652*(1), 48–69.

Southall, R. (2019). Polarization in South Africa: Toward Democratic Deepening or Democratic Decay? *The ANNALS of the American Academy of Political and Social Science, 681*(1), 194–208.

Stahler-Sholk, R. (2007). Resisting Neoliberal Homogenization: The Zapatista Autonomy Movement. *Latin American Perspectives, 34*(2), 48–63.

Stegmueller, D. (2011). Apples and Oranges? The Problem of Equivalence in Comparative Research. *Political Analysis, 19*(4), 471–487.

Stepan, A., & Skach, C. (1993). Constitutional Frameworks and Democratic Consolidation: Parliamentarianism versus Presidentialism. *World Politics, 46*(1), 1–22.

Stewart, A. J., McCarty, N., & Bryson, J. J. (2020). Polarization under Rising Inequality and Economic Decline. *Science Advances, 6*(50), eabd4201.

Stimson, J. A. (1991). *Public Opinion in America: Moods, Cycles, and Swings* (1st ed.). Westview Press.

Stimson, J. A. (2018). The Dyad Ratios Algorithm for Estimating Latent Public Opinion: Estimation, Testing, and Comparison to Other Approaches. *Bulletin of Sociological Methodology, 137–138*(1), 201–218.

Strom, K. (1986). Deferred Gratification and Minority Governments in Scandinavia. *Legislative Studies Quarterly, 11*(4), 583–605.

Svolik, M. W. (2020). When Polarization Trumps Civic Virtue: Partisan Conflict and the Subversion of Democracy by Incumbents. *Quarterly Journal of Political Science, 15*(1), 3–31.

Tai, Y., Hu, Y., & Solt, F. (2024). Democracy, Public Support, and Measurement Uncertainty. *American Political Science Review, 118*(1), 512–518.

Tajfel, H. (1982). Social Psychology of Intergroup Relations. *Annual Review of Psychology, 33*, 1–39.

Teorell, J., Dahlberg, S., Holmberg, S. et al. (2019). *The Quality of Government Standard Dataset.* The Quality of Government Institute, University of Gothenburg. Gothenburg, Sweden. www.qog.pol.gu.se.

Therborn, G. (2018). Twilight of Swedish Social Democracy. *New Left Review, 113*, 5–26.

Torcal, M., & Comellas, J. M. (2022). Affective Polarisation in Times of Political Instability and Conflict: Spain from a Comparative Perspective. *South European Society and Politics, 27*(1), 1–26.

Traber, D., Stoetzer, L. F., & Burri, T. (2023). Group-Based Public Opinion Polarisation in Multi-Party Systems. *West European Politics, 46*(4), 652–677.

Tworzecki, H. (2019). Poland: A Case of Top-Down Polarization. *The ANNALS of the American Academy of Political and Social Science, 681*(1), 97–119.

Voelkel, J. G., Chu, J., Stagnaro, M. N., Mernyk, J. S., et al. (2023). Interventions Reducing Affective Polarization Do Not Improve Anti-Democratic Attitudes. *Nature Human Behaviour, 7*(1), 55–64.

Voeten, E., & Brewer, P. R. (2006). Public Opinion, the War in Iraq, and Presidential Accountability. *Journal of Conflict Resolution, 50*(6), 809–830.

Voigt, L. (2019). Get the Party Started: The Social Policy of the Grand Coalition 2013–2017. *German Politics, 28*(3), 426–443.

Wagner, M. (2021). Affective Polarization in Multiparty Systems. *Electoral Studies, 69*, 102199.

Ward, D. G., & Tavits, M. (2019). How Partisan Affect Shapes Citizens' Perception of the Political World. *Electoral Studies, 60*, 1–9.

Weeks, J. (1986). An Interpretation of the Central American Crisis. *Latin American Research Review, 21*(3), 31–53.

Weisberg, H. F. (2005). *The Total Survey Error Approach: A Guide to the New Science of Survey Research*. The University of Chicago Press.

Weyland, K. (2020). Populism's Threat to Democracy: Comparative Lessons for the United States. *Perspectives on Politics, 18*(2), 389–406.

Wilder, D. A. (1978). Reduction of Intergroup Discrimination through Individuation of the Out-Group. *Journal of Personality and Social Psychology, 36*(12), 1361–1374.

Wirth, R. J., & Edwards, M. C. (2007). Item Factor Analysis: Current Approaches and Future Directions. *Psychological Methods, 12*(1), 58–79.

World Development Indicators. (2021). World Bank. Washington, DC. https://data.worldbank.org/indicator.

Xiao, Y. J., Coppin, G., & Van Bevel, J. J. (2016). Perceiving the World through Group-Colored Glasses: A Perceptual Model of Intergroup Relations. *Psychological Inquiry, 27*(4), 255–274.

Yeung, E. S., & Quek, K. (forthcoming). Self-Reported Political Ideology. *Political Science Research and Methods*.

Zaller, J. R. (1992). *The Nature and Origins of Mass Opinion*. Cambridge University Press.

Zechmeister, E. (2006). What's Left and Who's Right? A Q-Method Study of Individual and Contextual Influences on the Meaning of Ideological Labels. *Political Behavior, 28*(2), 151–173.

Zechmeister, E. J., & Corral, M. (2013). Individual and Contextual Constraints on Ideological Labels in Latin America. *Comparative Political Studies, 46*(6), 675–701.

Acknowledgments

For valuable comments and suggestions on many different stages of the project, I thank Santiago Olivella, Rahsaan Maxwell, Jim Adams, Izzy Laterzo, Nico De la Cerda, Ceci Martínez-Gallardo, Eric Guntermann, and three anonymous reviewers; participants at the 2021 APSA Annual Meeting and 2022 MPSA Annual Conference; and reading group participants at UC-Davis and UNC-Chapel Hill. Two others deserve special recognition. Marc Hetherington carefully read the entire manuscript and tolerated the distraction from my dissertation during my final year in graduate school. Randy Stevenson's enthusiasm for the project encouraged me to stick with it, and he provided meticulous feedback on how to improve the manuscript. I am indebted to him, Ray Duch, and Anja Neundorf for their excellent editorial guidance.

Some of the survey data used in the project was graciously made available by the Swiss Centre of Expertise in the Social Sciences, the Norwegian Centre for Research Data, and the Swedish National Data Service. I thank these organizations for their assistance. Short passages in Sections 1 and 2 were previously published open-access in Mehlhaff (2024b). I thank the *American Political Science Review* and Cambridge University Press for allowing the reprint of this content.

Cambridge Elements ≡

Comparative Political Behavior

Raymond Duch
University of Oxford

Raymond Duch is the co-founder and Director of the Centre for Experimental Social Sciences (CESS) at Nuffield College University of Oxford. He established and directed similar CESS centers in Chile, China, and India. He is also co-Director of the Candour Project that assembles a global team of research scholars with expertise in behavioral economics and data analytics addressing challenging health policy issues.

Anja Neundorf
University of Glasgow

Anja Neundorf is a Professor of Politics and Research Methods at the School of Social and Political Sciences at the University of Glasgow, UK. Before joining Glasgow, she held positions at the University of Nottingham (2013-2019) and Nuffield College, University of Oxford (2010-2012). She received her PhD from the University of Essex.

Randy Stevenson
Rice University

Randolph Stevenson is the Radoslav Tsanoff Professor of Public Affairs at Rice University in Houston, Texas. Professor Stevenson works and teaches in the areas of survey design, applied statistical methods, comparative mass political behavior, comparative political psychology, and experimental design.

About the Series

This Elements series is aimed at students and researchers interested in understanding how and why the political behaviour, perceptions, attitudes, emotional responses, interest, knowledge, and identities of citizens are conditioned on the political, social, and economic contexts in which they experience the political world.

Cambridge Elements⁼

Comparative Political Behavior

Elements in the Series

Conspiracy Theories and their Believers
Daniel Stockemer and Jean-Nicolas Bordeleau

Mass Polarization across Time and Space
Isaac D. Mehlhaff

A full series listing is available at: www.cambridge.org/ECPB

For EU product safety concerns, contact us at Calle de José Abascal, 56–1°,
28003 Madrid, Spain or eugpsr@cambridge.org.

www.ingramcontent.com/pod-product-compliance
Lightning Source LLC
LaVergne TN
LVHW020349260326
834688LV00045B/1622